1000
Coke or Pepsi
questions
2 ask your
friends!

coke OR pepsi?

Think you
and your
friends have
a lot in
common?

FINE print
PUBLISHING

Written and designed by
Mickey & Cheryl Gill

Fine Print Publishing Company
P.O. Box 916401
Longwood, Florida 32971-6401

ISBN 978-1-892951-38-0

This book is printed on acid-free paper.
Created in the U.S.A. & Printed in China

10 9 8 7

www.coke-or-pepsi.com

**Pass this book on to all your friends.
Each one gets to answer 40 crazy cool questions.**

**Soul-searching and sometimes silly questions reveal
what your friends are really made of!**

● Big Mac   ● Whopper?

Do you believe in love at first sight?   ■ yes ■ no

● *Social butterfly*   ● *Wallflower?*

■ Reality show   ■ Sitcom?

Answer a set of 40 questions and pass it back.

1. What is your full name? ...... Katherine M Vasquez

2. Nickname? ..... Katie

3. ◯ Coke ☑ Pepsi?

4. Favorite song? ...... So what

5. Earliest memory? ...... in my crib

6. ◯ Milk ☑ Dark chocolate?

7. Who do you call when you're upset? ...... my best friend

8. Do you recycle? ☑ yes ☐ no

9. ☑ Big Mac ◯ Whopper?

10. Last book you read? ...... the sight. Warriors

11. ◯ Beach ☑ Mountains?

12. What kind of shoes are you wearing? ...... converes

13. ☑ TV ◯ Book?

14. Favorite store? ...... J.K. rose

15. What was the last thing you ate? ...... pasta & bread stick

16. ☑ Clean freak ◯ Total slob?

17. Favorite car? ...... slug bug

18. Best gift you've ever received? ...... a brand new bike

19. Best gift you've ever given? ...... webkinz

20. Do you wish on ★ ★ ★ ? yes ☑ no ☐

21. Ever been stung by a jellyfish? ☐ yes ☑ no

22. Best cartoon ever? *scooby doo*

23. What scares you? *singled out*

24. Last person you spoke to? *Eileen*

25. Favorite doughnut? *sugar*

26. Stupidest thing you've ever done? *climb on a swinging rope*

27. Been to NYC? ☑ yes ☐ no

28. Best sitcom ever? *?*

29. Been to LA? ☐ yes ☑ no

30. Favorite place you've visited? *NYC*

31. Least favorite vegetable? *asparagis*

32. ☑ Dreamer ◯ Doer?

33. One word to describe you? *indapendant*

34. Name of your very first friend? *no clue*

35. If I could, I would change my first name to *Sammantha*

36. ◯ Night light ☑ Completely dark?

37. Ever pull an all-nighter? *no*

38. Believe in love at first sight? ☐ yes ☑ no

39. Best toppings for pizza? *canadian baccon, cheese, pinapple*

40. Ever owned a goldfish? ☑ yes name *Flames* ☐ no

1. Name given at birth? _Melissa cai_

2. What do your friends call you? _Melissa_

3. What do you do when you're mad? _cry/scream_

4. Favorite holiday and why? _chrismas/ gift_

5. Ever won anything? ☑ yeah What? _Hall of fame_ ☐ nah

6. What do you do on rainy days? ☂ _wear rain coat_

7. 🐕 ⚫ 🐈 ⚪ person?

8. Favorite flower? _rose_

9. ⚪ Coffee ⚫ Tea?

10. Oldest living relative: 👴 Name _grandpa_ Age _70_

11. Most annoying bug? _none_

12. ⚪ Tanning oil ⚫ Sunscreen?

13. Nails: ⚫ Painted ⚪ Chipped ⚪ Fake ⚪ Bitten?

14. Wear painful shoes just because they're cute? ☑ yeah ☐ nah

15. Best type of music? _none_

16. Ever been in love? ☐ yeah ☑ nah

17. Favorite actor? _Zac Efront/Miley Cyrus_

18. ⚪ Radio ⚫ iPod?

19. Favorite actress? _Vanessa Hudgens/Miley Cyrus_

20. Do you have a secret you've never told anyone? ☑ yeah ☐ nah

21. Did you ever believe in the Tooth Fairy? ☑ *yeah* ☐ *nah*

22. Favorite thing to nosh on? <u>pizza</u>

23. Mall ◯ Outlet

24. Your absolute favorite article of clothing? <u>none</u>

25. ◯ Frozen yogurt ● Ice cream?

26. What superpower would you love to have? <u>fly</u>

27. ● Potato chips ● French fries?

28. Cosmetic you can't live without? <u>make up</u>

29. Best teacher you ever had? <u>Mrs. Nicholson</u>

30. ◯ Spender ● Saver?

31. Who should play you in a movie version of your life? <u>don't know</u>

32. If you were an animal, what would you be? <u>dog</u>

33. Best beverage? <u>sprite</u>

34. Favorite cereal? <u>muchmello magice</u>

35. Who do you wish you could meet? <u>a princess</u>

36. 😨 ◯ Fearful 😀 ● Fearless?

37. Which would you try? ◯ Skydiving ◯ Rappelling ● Scuba Diving

38. ● Butterflies ◯ Dragonflies?

39. ● Organic ◯ Junk food?

40. Favorite school subject? <u>science</u>

1. What's your full name? Shea Lynn Cooke

2. Elementary school: ☐ Bully ☑ Bullied?

3. Dream job? actor

4. Glass: ☑ ½ full ○ ½ empty?

5. Ever broken a body part? ☐ Yep What? . . . . ☑ Nope

6. How many car accidents have you been in? 0

7. Ever caused a car accident? ○ Yep ☑ Nope

8. Ever been sent to the principal's office? ☐ Yep ☑ Nope

9. Most beautiful (inside) person you know? Mykenzie Genti

10. How do you relax? play video game

11. ☑ Social butterfly ○ Wallflower?

12. Your biggest question about life? What Will Global

out the human race
13. ☑ Secret keeper ☐ Blabbermouth? Warming Wipe

14. What makes you cry? Pain and being bullied

15. Names of future children? Boy Gerrit Girl Patonia

16. Who's your favorite relative? Grandma

17. What was your last dream? ;

18. What makes you crazy? rapid talking

19. I wish I could fly

20. ○ Stick shift ○ Automatic ☑ Can't drive yet?

21. Which appointment is worse? ☐ Doctor ☑ Dentist

22. Ever been to the emergency room? ◯ Yes ⊘ No

23. ☑ Worry wart ☐ Worry free?

24. ⊘ Bicycle through Europe ◯ African safari?

25. Favorite food court place? ... Mc Donalds ......

26. ☑ Ice cubes ☐ Crushed ice?

27. What do you like on your burger? .... meat and cheese

28. Favorite fast food? ...... Mc Donalds

29. Favorite color of eyes? ...... blue

30. Do you know sign language? ◯ YES ⊘ NO

31. Favorite department store? .. Claire's

32. Who taught you to ride a bike? 🚲 .. my dad

33. How old were you when you learned to swim? .... 3 years

34. I would love to try .. to scuba dive

35. Who do you admire most? .. my mom

36. ☐ Bikini ☑ Board shorts?

37. Worst movie ever? ... Space Chimps

38. Favorite kind of cookie? ... Peanut butter

39. Best commercial? 📺 ....

40. A word or phrase you say a lot? ....

1. First, middle, and last name? Eileen_ Cai

2. I can't live without _My_ parents_

3. Do you take vitamins? ☐ uh, yeah ☒ um, no

4. Do you floss? ☐ uh, yeah ☒ um, no

5. How many hair products do you use? ☐ 1 ☐ 2 ☒ 3 ☐ ?

6. Meanest thing you ever did to a sibling? _ kick her_ in the fa

7. Believe in UFOs? ☐ uh, yeah ☒ um, no

8. Can you identify constellations? ☐ uh, yeah ☒ um, no

9. ☒ Creamy ☐ Crunchy Peanut Butter?

10. Someone you miss? dad

11. Believe in the Loch Ness Monster? ☐ uh, yeah ☒ um, no

12. Believe in Big Foot? ☐ uh, yeah ☒ um, no

13. Which would you pick? can't pick ☐ Extra $50 a week ☐ 3-day weekend

14. Any pets? ☐ uh, yeah _____ ☒ um, no
(kind)

15. If yes to #14, Names _____

16. Museum of ☒ art ☐ Natural history?

17. ☒ Train ☐ Plane ☐ Automobile?

18. I wish my hair _ was_ brown_ and straight

19. Best amusement park ride? _water_ roller_ coaster, roll
coaster

20. Best little kid movie? _ I _ don't_ have_ one

21. FAVORITE PICTURE BOOK? _none_ _ _ _ _ _

22. ☒ APPLES ☐ ORANGES?

23. ☐ CHOCOLATE MILK ☒ SOY MILK ☐ RICE MILK?

24. ☐ HOT DOG ☒ HAMBURGER?

25. I WISH SOMEONE WOULD INVENT _a time machine_

26. ☐ WHITE ☒ WHEAT?

27. BEST ERA FOR FASHION? ☐ '60S ☐ '70S ☐ '80S ☐ '90S ☐ NOW

28. HOW MANY HOURS PER DAY ONLINE? _about 2-5 hours_

29. HOW MANY HOURS PER DAY ON PHONE? _about 10min. - 1 hour_

30. JUST SAY NO TO _ _ _ _ _ _ _ _ _ _ _ _ _ _

31. ☒ FLIP-FLOPS ☐ STRAPPY SANDALS?

32. BEST FOOD COMES FROM WHICH COUNTRY? _ _ _ _ _ _ _

33. RUN AWAY FROM HOME WHEN YOU WERE LITTLE? ☐ UH, YEAH ☒ UM, NO

34. WHAT'S SCARIER? ☐ SNAKE ☒ SHARK

35. WHAT ARE YOU NOT GOOD AT? _fear at bugs_ _ _ _

36. FRIEND YOU'VE HAD THE LONGEST? _Julia_ _ _ _ _

37. FRIEND WHO LIVES THE FARTHEST FROM YOU? _Julia, cousins_

38. WHERE DOES # 37 FRIEND LIVE? _ _ _ _ _ _ _ _

39. HOW MANY HOURS PER DAY WATCHING TV? _0min. - 3 hours_

40. WHICH ONE COULD YOU GIVE UP? ☐ E-MAIL ☐ CELL PHONE
I cant give up

? yin
feet planted on the ground
c a l m

1. First, middle, and last name? _Melissa Caine_ a Cai

2. What toothpaste do you use? _Hello kitty bubble gum_

3. ◯ Shop alone ● Shop with mom ◯ Shop with friends?

4. Best type of cake? _Choclate_

5. I love the smell of _strabierries_

6. How do you like your popcorn? _Buttery_

7. Favorite magazine? _American girl_

8. ◯ Aspirin ◯ Aceteminifin ◯ Ibuprofen ◯ Tough it out?

9. What did you do last night? _play webkinz_

10. ◯ Manicure ◯ Do-it-yourself nails?

11. What's your favorite comfort food? _____

12. ● High fashion ◯ Total casual?

13. ◯ Kill bugs ● Try to save them?

14. Best friend in kindergarten? _Didi, Michelle_

15. I can't bear the sound of _Vacume_

16. What was your favorite thing on the playground? _Swing_

17. I would love to see _the president's House_

18. I would love to time-travel back to _When I was a baby_

19. I would love to time-travel forward to _I'm twelv._

20. Can you change a tire? ◯ Yes ● No

21. Swallow anything by accident as a kid? ● Yes _gum_ (what) ○ No

22. ○ Romantic dinner for two ● Big party?

23. Favorite take-out food? _Sunny-D_

24. I can't stand the smell of _Dump_

25. Favorite smoothie? _straberry_

26. Ever tried dog or cat food? ○ Yes ● No

27. Hair color? _Dark brown_

28. 👀 ○ Contacts ○ Glasses ● Great vision?

29. Favorite game as a kid? _House_

30. ○ Salty ● Sweet?

31. I can't wait until I can _go outside myself_

32. ○ Lone Ranger ● Team player?

33. Do you try to find shapes in clouds? ● Yes ○ No

34. ● Details ○ Big picture?

35. What are you good at? _gymnastics_

36. Favorite accessory? _necklece_

37. ● Appointment for color ○ Dye your own hair?

38. I love to listen to _music_

39. Coolest thing you learned this week? _twirlers_

40. ○ Tap ○ Bottled ● Sparkling water?

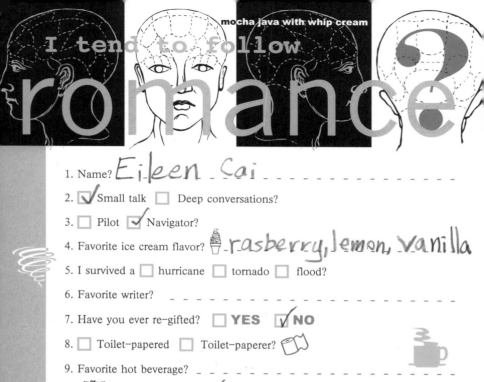

mocha java with whip cream

I tend to follow

romance?

1. Name? Eileen Cai

2. ☑ Small talk ☐ Deep conversations?

3. ☐ Pilot ☑ Navigator?

4. Favorite ice cream flavor? rasberry, lemon, vanilla

5. I survived a ☐ hurricane ☐ tornado ☐ flood?

6. Favorite writer? _ _ _ _ _ _ _ _ _

7. Have you ever re-gifted? ☐ **YES** ☑ **NO**

8. ☐ Toilet-papered ☐ Toilet-paperer?

9. Favorite hot beverage? _ _ _ _ _ _

10. ⏰ Time ☐ drags ☑ goes by too fast?

11. Most influential person in your life? _ _ _ _ _ _ _ _

12. Who would you be in a castle? ☑ Queen ☐ Princess ☐ Knight ☐ Jester

13. What do you daydream about? ☺ _ _ _ _ _ _ _

14. ☑ Meat eater ☐ Vegetarian ☐ Vegan?

15. Habit you wish you could change? _ _ _ _ _ _

16. Best type of movie? ☐ Romance ☐ Comedy ☐ Scary ☑ Action ☐ Sci-Fi

17. Any advice for a 5-year-old? read _ _ _ _ _ _

18. ☑ Reality show ☐ Sitcom?

19. Birthday? July 12th 1998 _ _ _ _ _ _

20. ☐ Bagel ☑ Doughnut ☑ Croissant ☐ Cinnamon roll?

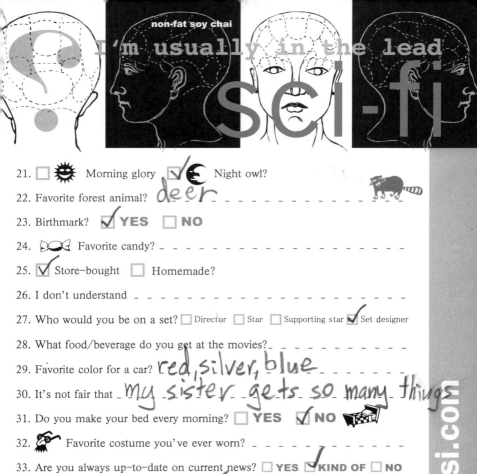

non-fat soy chai

I'm usually in the lead

sci-fi

21. ☐ ☀ Morning glory ☑ 🌙 Night owl?

22. Favorite forest animal? deer _ _ _ _ _ _ _ _ _ _

23. Birthmark? ☑ YES ☐ NO

24. 🍬 Favorite candy? _ _ _ _ _ _ _ _ _ _ _ _

25. ☑ Store-bought ☐ Homemade?

26. I don't understand _ _ _ _ _ _ _ _ _ _ _ _

27. Who would you be on a set? ☐ Director ☐ Star ☐ Supporting star ☑ Set designer

28. What food/beverage do you get at the movies? _ _ _ _ _ _ _ _ _ _

29. Favorite color for a car? red, silver, blue _ _ _ _ _ _ _

30. It's not fair that _ my sister gets so many things

31. Do you make your bed every morning? ☐ YES ☑ NO 🗒

32. 👓 Favorite costume you've ever worn? _ _ _ _ _ _ _ _ _ _

33. Are you always up-to-date on current news? ☐ YES ☑ KIND OF ☐ NO

34. ☐ Waffle cone ☐ Sugar cone ☑ Cup?

35. Which is worse? ☐ No TV ☑ No music

36. ☑ Small purse ☐ Giant bag?

37. Favorite fairy tale? _ _ _ _ _ _ _ _ _ _ _ _ _ _ _

38. Ever have an imaginary friend? ☐ YES _ _ _ _ _ _ _ ☑ NO
                                              (Name)

39. Can different foods touch each other on your plate? ☐ YES ☑ NO

40. Best jungle animal? _ _ _ _ _ _ _ _ _ _ _ _ _ _ _

sweet

wind on my face

1. Name _Melissa_ Where were you born? _Here_

2. Sit ● up front ○ in the back?

3. Favorite toy when you were a kid? _Webkinz_

4. Which is worse? ○ Shopping for jeans ● Shopping for bikini

5. Favorite season and why? _Spring because its my birthday._

6. Do you read the ending before you finish a book? ○ Yes ● No

7. Best brand of jeans? _Limited too_

8. ○ Island cabana ○ European castle ○ Safari tent ● Ski lodge

9. Favorite color combination? _blue, pink_

10. ○ Sunset ● Sunrise?

11. Favorite number? _54_ Why? _Just cause_

12. Color your toes are painted? _____

13. Ever needed stitches? ○ Yes Why? _____ ● No

14. My favorite shoes are _flip flop_

15. ● Right-handed ○ Left-handed ○ Ambidextrous?

16. How many children would you like someday? _____

17. ○ Tent ○ Cabin?

18. What scared you as a kid? _____

19. For just a day, I would switch places with _____

20. Wake up to ○ alarm ○ radio?

21. Been in a talent show? ⚪ Yes Talent? _____ No ●

22. ⚪ Go with the flow ● Stick to a routine?

23. Coolest first name? _Gabreilla_

24. ● Polka dots ⚪ Stripes ⚪ Plaid ⚪ Paisley?

25. Coolest last name? _Montez_

26. ⚪ Paper ● Plastic?

27. What can you draw well? _girls_

28. ● Brownies ⚪ Chocolate chip cookies

29. I will not eat _spicy stuff_

30. ● Gold ⚪ Silver?

31. Favorite hangout? _Build-a-Bear Workshop_

32. How many times have you moved in your life? _Six_

33. As a kid, ● stuffed animal ⚪ blankie?

34. Favorite thing to do on the weekend? _Watch a Move_

35. What color is your bedroom? _White_

36. ● Mild ⚪ Spicy?

37. What would be hard to give up? _My Parents_

38. Cutest thing your pet does? _Do not have pet_

39. ⚪ Shower ● Bath?

40. I have a problem with _Waiting for my B-da_

1. What is your full name? Melissa Cai

2. Nickname? Mer Mei

3. ○ Coke ● Pepsi?

4. Favorite song? Wamanizer, Love Story

5. Earliest memory? Watching Hotel for Dogs

6. ○ Milk ● Dark chocolate?

7. Who do you call when you're upset? My Mom

8. Do you recycle? ✷ ☒ yes ☐ no

9. ● Big Mac ○ Whopper?

10. Last book you read? Goldie

11. ● Beach ○ Mountains?

12. What kind of shoes are you wearing? HEELYS

13. ● TV ○ Book?

14. Favorite store? LibbyLu, Clarie's

15. What was the last thing you ate? Sandwich

16. ● Clean freak ○ Total slob?

17. Favorite car? None

18. Best gift you've ever received? A Make up Kit

19. Best gift you've ever given? Webkinz

20. Do you wish on ★ ★ ★ ? yes ☒ no ☐

21. Ever been stung by a jellyfish? ☐ yes ☐ no

22. Best cartoon ever? . . . .

23. What scares you? . . . .

24. Last person you spoke to? . . . .

25. Favorite doughnut? . . . .

26. Stupidest thing you've ever done? . . . .

27. Been to NYC? ☐ yes ☐ no

28. Best sitcom ever? . . . .

29. Been to LA? ☐ yes ☐ no

30. Favorite place you've visited? . . . .

31. Least favorite vegetable? . . . .

32. ◯ Dreamer ◯ Doer?

33. One word to describe you? . . . .

34. Name of your very first friend? . . . .

35. If I could, I would change my first name to . . . .

36. ◯ Night light ◯ Completely dark?

37. Ever pull an all-nighter? . . . .

38. Believe in love at first sight? ☐ yes ☐ no

39. Best toppings for pizza? . . . .

40. Ever owned a goldfish? ☐ yes name . . . . ☐ no

coke-or-pepsi.com

1. Name given at birth? _Melissa Cai_
2. What do your friends call you? _Melissa_
3. What do you do when you're mad? _shout and cry_
4. Favorite holiday and why? _Christmas because we get present_
5. Ever won anything? ☐ *yeah* What? _____ ☑ *nah*
6. What do you do on rainy days? ☂ _Where Big long coats_
7. 🐻 🐈 ○ person?
8. Favorite flower? _Rose, Buttercup_
9. ○ Coffee ◉ Tea?
10. Oldest living relative: Name _grandpa_ Age _75_
11. Most annoying bug? _Moth, Fly_
12. ○ Tanning oil ◉ Sunscreen?
13. Nails: ◉ Painted ○ Chipped ◉ Fake ○ Bitten?
14. Wear painful shoes just because they're cute? ☑ *yeah* ☐ *nah*
15. Best type of music? _Fast_
16. Ever been in love? ☐ *yeah* ☑ *nah*
17. Favorite actor? _Zac Efron_
18. ○ Radio ◉ iPod?
19. Favorite actress? _Vanessa Hedgens_
20. Do you have a secret you've never told anyone? ☑ *yeah* ☐ *nah*

cool

21. Did you ever believe in the Tooth Fairy? ☐ yeah ☐ nah

22. Favorite thing to nosh on? _____

23. ◯ Mall ◯ Outlet

24. Your absolute favorite article of clothing? _____

25. ◯ Frozen yogurt ◯ Ice cream?

26. What superpower would you love to have? _____

27. ◯ Potato chips ◯ French fries?

28. Cosmetic you can't live without? _____

29. Best teacher you ever had? _____

30. ◯ Spender ◯ Saver?

31. Who should play you in a movie version of your life? _____

32. If you were an animal, what would you be? _____

33. Best beverage? _____

34. Favorite cereal? _____

35. Who do you wish you could meet? _____

36. ◯ Fearful ◯ Fearless?

37. Which would you try? ◯ Skydiving ◯ Rappelling ◯ Scuba Diving

38. ◯ Butterflies ◯ Dragonflies?

39. ◯ Organic ◯ Junk food?

40. Favorite school subject? _____

coke-or-pepsi.com

1. What's your full name? *Melissa Cai*
2. Elementary school: ☐ Bully ☑ Bullied?
3. Dream job? *Designer*
4. Glass: ☑ ½ full ☐ ½ empty?
5. Ever broken a body part? ☐ Yep What? .... ☑ Nope
6. How many car accidents have you been in? *None*
7. Ever caused a car accident? ☐ Yep ☑ Nope
8. Ever been sent to the principal's office? ☐ Yep ☑ Nope
9. Most beautiful (inside) person you know? *My parents*
10. How do you relax? *sewing a pillow*
11. ☑ Social butterfly ☐ Wallflower?
12. Your biggest question about life? *None*
13. ☑ Secret keeper ☐ Blabbermouth?
14. What makes you cry? *Getting Hit*
15. Names of future children? Boy *Joshua* Girl *Crysta*
16. Who's your favorite relative? *All*
17. What was your last dream? *None*
18. What makes you crazy? *Barfing*
19. I wish I *could have my own kids*
20. ☐ Stick shift ☐ Automatic ☑ Can't drive yet?

21. Which appointment is worse? ☐ Doctor ☐ Dentist

22. Ever been to the emergency room? ◯ Yes ◯ No

23. ☐ Worry wart ☐ Worry free?

24. ◯ Bicycle through Europe ◯ African safari?

25. Favorite food court place? . . . .

26. ☐ Ice cubes ☐ Crushed ice?

27. 🥫 What do you like on your burger? . . . .

28. Favorite fast food? . . . .

29. Favorite color of eyes? . . . .

30. Do you know sign language? ◯ 🤟YE🤘S ◯ ✊N👋O

31. Favorite department store? . . . .

32. Who taught you to ride a bike? 🚲 . . . .

33. How old were you when you learned to swim? . . . .

34. I would love to try . . . .

35. Who do you admire most? . . . .

36. ☐ Bikini ☐ Board shorts?

37. Worst movie ever? . . . .

38. Favorite kind of cookie? . . . .

39. Best commercial? 📺 . . . .

40. A word or phrase you say a lot? . . . .

coke-or-pepsi.com

1. First, middle, and last name? _ _ _ _ _ _ _ _ _ _ _ _ _ _ _ _

2. I can't live without _

3. Do you take vitamins? ☐ uh, yeah ☐ um, no

4. Do you floss? ☐ uh, yeah ☐ um, no

5. How many hair products do you use? ☐ 1 ☐ 2 ☐ 3 ☐ ?

6. Meanest thing you ever did to a sibling? _ _ _ _ _ _ _ _ _ .

7. Believe in UFOs? ☐ uh, yeah ☐ um, no

8. Can you identify constellations? ☐ uh, yeah ☐ um, no

9. ☐ Creamy ☐ Crunchy Peanut Butter?

10. Someone you miss? _

11. Believe in the Loch Ness Monster? ☐ uh, yeah ☐ um, no

12. Believe in Big Foot? ☐ uh, yeah ☐ um, no

13. Which would you pick? ☐ Extra $50 a week ☐ 3-day weekend

14. Any pets? ☐ uh, yeah _ _ _ _ _ _ _ _ _ _ _ _ ☐ um, no
                              (kind)

15. If yes to #14, names _ _ _ _ _ _ _ _ _ _ _ _ _ _ _ _ _ _

16. Museum of ☐ art ☐ natural history?

17. ☐ Train ☐ Plane ☐ Automobile?

18. I wish my hair _

19. Best amusement park ride? _ _ _ _ _ _ _ _ _ _ _ _ _ _ _ _

20. Best little kid movie? _ _ _ _ _ _ _ _ _ _ _ _ _ _ _ _ _

21. FAVORITE PICTURE BOOK? _ _ _ _ _ _ _ _ _ _ _ _ _ _ _ _

22. ☐ APPLES ☐ ORANGES?

23. ☐ CHOCOLATE MILK ☐ SOY MILK ☐ RICE MILK?

24. ☐ HOT DOG ☐ HAMBURGER?

25. I WISH SOMEONE WOULD INVENT _ _ _ _ _ _ _ _ _ _ _ _ _ _

26. ☐ WHITE ☐ WHEAT?

27. BEST ERA FOR FASHION? ☐ '60S ☐ '70S ☐ '80S ☐ '90S ☐ NOW

28. HOW MANY HOURS PER DAY ONLINE? _ _ _ _ _ _ _ _ _ _

29. HOW MANY HOURS PER DAY ON PHONE? _ _ _ _ _ _ _ _ _

30. JUST SAY NO TO _ _ _ _ _ _ _ _ _ _ _ _ _ _ _ _ _ _

31. ☐ FLIP-FLOPS ☐ STRAPPY SANDALS?

32. BEST FOOD COMES FROM WHICH COUNTRY? _ _ _ _ _ _ _ _ _

33. RUN AWAY FROM HOME WHEN YOU WERE LITTLE? ☐ UH, YEAH ☐ UM, NO

34. WHAT'S SCARIER? ☐ SNAKE ☐ SHARK

35. WHAT ARE YOU NOT GOOD AT? _ _ _ _ _ _ _ _ _ _ _ _

36. FRIEND YOU'VE HAD THE LONGEST? _ _ _ _ _ _ _ _ _ _

37. FRIEND WHO LIVES THE FARTHEST FROM YOU? _ _ _ _ _ _ _

38. WHERE DOES # 37 FRIEND LIVE? _ _ _ _ _ _ _ _ _ _

39. HOW MANY HOURS PER DAY WATCHING TV? _ _ _ _ _ _ _ _

40. WHICH ONE COULD YOU GIVE UP? ☐ E-MAIL ☐ CELL PHONE

coke-or-pepsi.com

?
yin
feet planted on the ground
c a l m

1. First, middle, and last name? _____

2. What toothpaste do you use? _____

3. ◯ Shop alone ◯ Shop with mom ◯ Shop with friends?

4. Best type of cake? _____

5. I love the smell of _____

6. How do you like your popcorn? _____

7. Favorite magazine? _____

8. ◯ Aspirin ◯ Aceteminifin ◯ Ibuprofen ◯ Tough it out?

9. What did you do last night? _____

10. ◯ Manicure ◯ Do-it-yourself nails?

11. What's your favorite comfort food? _____

12. ◯ High fashion ◯ Total casual?

13. ◯ Kill bugs ◯ Try to save them?

14. Best friend in kindergarten? _____

15. I can't bear the sound of _____

16. What was your favorite thing on the playground? _____

17. I would love to see _____

18. I would love to time-travel back to _____

19. I would love to time-travel forward to _____

20. Can you change a tire? ◯ Yes ◯ No

...yang?
head in the clouds
c h a o s

21. Swallow anything by accident as a kid? ◯ Yes _____ ◯ No
    (what)

22. ◯ Romantic dinner for two ◯ Big party?

23. Favorite take-out food? _____

24. I can't stand the smell of [icon] _____

25. Favorite smoothie? _____

26. Ever tried dog or cat food? ◯ Yes ◯ No

27. Hair color? _____

28. [eyes icon] ◯ Contacts ◯ Glasses ◯ Great vision?

29. Favorite game as a kid? _____

30. ◯ Salty ◯ Sweet?

31. I can't wait until I can _____

32. ◯ Lone Ranger ◯ Team player?

33. Do you try to find shapes in clouds? ◯ Yes ◯ No [cloud icon]

34. ◯ Details ◯ Big picture?

35. What are you good at? _____

36. [necklace icon] Favorite accessory? _____

37. ◯ Appointment for color ◯ Dye your own hair? [CD icon]

38. I love to listen to _____

39. Coolest thing you learned this week? _____

40. ◯ Tap ◯ Bottled ◯ Sparkling water?

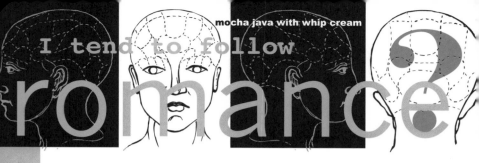

I tend to follow **romance**?

mocha java with whip cream

1. Name? _

2. ☐ Small talk ☐ Deep conversations?

3. ☐ Pilot ☐ Navigator?

4. Favorite ice cream flavor? _ _ _ _ _ _ _ _ _ _ _ _ _ _

5. I survived a ☐ hurricane ☐ tornado ☐ flood?

6. Favorite writer? _ _ _ _ _ _ _ _ _ _ _ _ _ _ _

7. Have you ever re-gifted? ☐ **YES** ☐ **NO**

8. ☐ Toilet-papered ☐ Toilet-paperer?

9. Favorite hot beverage? _ _ _ _ _ _ _ _ _ _ _ _ _ _ _ _ _ _

10. ☐ Time ☐ drags ☐ goes by too fast?

11. Most influential person in your life? _ _ _ _ _ _ _ _ _ _ _ _

12. Who would you be in a castle? ☐ Queen ☐ Princess ☐ Knight ☐ Jester

13. What do you daydream about? _ _ _ _ _ _ _ _ _ _ _ _ _ _

14. ☐ Meat eater ☐ Vegetarian ☐ Vegan?

15. Habit you wish you could change? _ _ _ _ _ _ _ _ _ _ _ _

16. Best type of movie? ☐ Romance ☐ Comedy ☐ Scary ☐ Action ☐ Sci-Fi

17. Any advice for a 5-year-old? _ _ _ _ _ _ _ _ _ _ _ _ _ _

18. ☐ Reality show ☐ Sitcom?

19. Birthday? _ _ _ _ _ _ _ _ _ _ _ _ _ _ _ _ _ _

20. ☐ Bagel ☐ Doughnut ☐ Croissant ☐ Cinnamon roll?

21. ☐ ☀ Morning glory ☐ ☾ Night owl?

22. Favorite forest animal? _

23. Birthmark? ☐ **YES** ☐ **NO**

24. 🍬 Favorite candy? _ _ _ _ _ _ _ _ _ _ _ _ _ _ _ _ _ _

25. ☐ Store-bought ☐ Homemade?

26. I don't understand _

27. Who would you be on a set? ☐ Director ☐ Star ☐ Supporting star ☐ Set designer

28. What food/beverage do you get at the movies? _ _ _ _ _ _ _ _ _

29. Favorite color for a car? _ _ _ _ _ _ _ _ _ _ _ _ _ _ _

30. It's not fair that _

31. Do you make your bed every morning? ☐ **YES** ☐ **NO** 🛏

32. 👓 Favorite costume you've ever worn? _ _ _ _ _ _ _ _ _ _ _ _

33. Are you always up-to-date on current news? ☐ **YES** ☐ **KIND OF** ☐ **NO**

34. ☐ Waffle cone ☐ Sugar cone ☐ Cup?

35. Which is worse? ☐ No TV ☐ No music

36. ☐ Small purse ☐ Giant bag?

37. Favorite fairy tale? _

38. Ever have an imaginary friend? ☐ **YES** _ _ _ _ _ _ _ _ _ _ _ ☐ **NO**
    (Name)

39. Can different foods touch each other on your plate? ☐ **YES** ☐ **NO**

🐒 40. Best jungle animal? _ _ _ _ _ _ _ _ _ _ _ _ _ _ _ _ _ _

1. Name _____ Where were you born? _____

2. Sit ⭕ up front ⭕ in the back?

3. Favorite toy when you were a kid? _____

4. Which is worse? ⭕ Shopping for jeans ⭕ Shopping for bikini

5. Favorite season and why? _____

6. Do you read the ending before you finish a book? ⭕ Yes ⭕ No

7. Best brand of jeans? _____

8. ⭕ Island cabana ⭕ European castle ⭕ Safari tent ⭕ Ski lodge

9. Favorite color combination? _____

10. ⭕ Sunset ⭕ Sunrise?

11. Favorite number? _____ Why? _____

12. Color your toes are painted? _____

13. Ever needed stitches? ⭕ Yes Why? _____ ⭕ No

14. My favorite shoes are _____

15. ⭕ Right-handed ⭕ Left-handed ⭕ Ambidextrous?

16. How many children would you like someday? _____

17. ⭕ Tent ⭕ Cabin?

18. What scared you as a kid? _____

19. For just a day, I would switch places with _____

20. Wake up to ⭕ alarm ⭕ radio?

21. Been in a talent show? ◯ Yes Talent? _____ No ◯

22. ◯ Go with the flow ◯ Stick to a routine?

23. Coolest first name? _____

24. ◯ Polka dots ◯ Stripes ◯ Plaid ◯ Paisley?

25. Coolest last name? _____

26. ◯ Paper ◯ Plastic?

27. What can you draw well? _____

28. ◯ Brownies ◯ Chocolate chip cookies

29. I will not eat _____

30. ◯ Gold ◯ Silver?

31. Favorite hangout? _____

32. How many times have you moved in your life? _____

33. As a kid, ◯ stuffed animal ◯ blankie?

34. Favorite thing to do on the weekend? _____

35. What color is your bedroom? _____

36. ◯ Mild ◯ Spicy?

37. What would be hard to give up? _____

38. Cutest thing your pet does? _____

39. ◯ Shower ◯ Bath?

40. I have a problem with _____

bittersweet

secret

my room is a total mess

NO PARKING

1. What is your full name? . . . .

2. Nickname? . . . .

3. ◯ Coke ◯ Pepsi?

4. Favorite song? . . . .

5. Earliest memory? . . . .

6. ◯ Milk ◯ Dark chocolate?

7. Who do you call when you're upset? . . . .

8. Do you recycle? ♻ ☐ yes ☐ no

9. ◯ Big Mac ◯ Whopper?

10. Last book you read? . . . .

11. ◯ 🏖 Beach ◯ ⛰ Mountains?

12. What kind of shoes are you wearing? . . . .

13. ◯ TV ◯ Book?

14. Favorite store? . . . .

15. What was the last thing you ate? 🍜 . . . .

16. ◯ Clean freak ◯ Total slob?

17. Favorite car? . . . .

18. Best gift you've ever received? . . . .

19. Best gift you've ever given? . . . .

20. Do you wish on ★ ★ ★ ? yes ☐ no ☐

21. Ever been stung by a jellyfish? ☐ yes ☐ no

22. Best cartoon ever? . . . .

23. What scares you? . . . .

24. Last person you spoke to? . . . .

25. Favorite doughnut? . . . .

26. Stupidest thing you've ever done? . . . .

27. Been to NYC? ☐ yes ☐ no

28. Best sitcom ever? . . . .

29. Been to LA? ☐ yes ☐ no

30. Favorite place you've visited? . . . .

31. Least favorite vegetable? . . . .

32. ◯ Dreamer ◯ Doer?

33. One word to describe you? . . . .

34. Name of your very first friend? . . . .

35. If I could, I would change my first name to . . . .

36. ◯ Night light ◯ Completely dark?

37. Ever pull an all-nighter? . . . .

38. Believe in love at first sight? ☐ yes ☐ no

39. Best toppings for pizza? . . . .

40. Ever owned a goldfish? ☐ yes name . . . . ☐ no

coke-or-pepsi.com

1. Name given at birth? _____

2. What do your friends call you? _____

3. What do you do when you're mad? _____

4. Favorite holiday and why? _____

5. Ever won anything? ☐ yeah What? _____ ☐ nah

6. What do you do on rainy days? ☂ _____

7. 🐆 ◯ 🐈 ◯ person?

8. Favorite flower? _____

9. ◯ Coffee ◯ Tea?

10. Oldest living relative: 🧓 Name _____ Age _____

11. Most annoying bug? _____

12. ◯ Tanning oil ◯ Sunscreen?

13. Nails: ◯ Painted ◯ Chipped ◯ Fake ◯ Bitten?

14. Wear painful shoes just because they're cute? ☐ yeah ☐ nah

15. Best type of music? _____

16. Ever been in love? ☐ yeah ☐ nah

17. Favorite actor? _____

18. ◯ Radio ◯ iPod?

19. Favorite actress? _____

20. Do you have a secret you've never told anyone? ☐ yeah ☐ nah

21. Did you ever believe in the Tooth Fairy? ☐ yeah ☐ nah

22.  Favorite thing to nosh on? _____

23. ◯ Mall ◯ Outlet

24. Your absolute favorite article of clothing? _____

25. ◯ Frozen yogurt ◯ Ice cream?

26. What superpower would you love to have? _____

27. ◯ Potato chips ◯ French fries?

28. Cosmetic you can't live without? _____

29. Best teacher you ever had? _____

30. ◯ Spender ◯ Saver?

31. Who should play you in a movie version of your life? _____

32. If you were an animal, what would you be? _____

33. Best beverage? _____

34. Favorite cereal? _____

35. Who do you wish you could meet? _____

36. ◯ Fearful ◯ Fearless?

37. Which would you try? ◯ Skydiving ◯ Rappelling ◯ Scuba Diving

38. ◯ Butterflies ◯ Dragonflies?

39. ◯ Organic ◯ Junk food?

40. Favorite school subject? _____

coke-or-pepsi.com

1. What's your full name? . . . .

2. Elementary school: ☐ Bully ☐ Bullied?

3. Dream job? . . . .

4. Glass: ○ ½ full ○ ½ empty?

5. Ever broken a body part? ☐ Yep What? . . . . ☐ Nope

6. How many car accidents have you been in? . . . .

7. Ever caused a car accident? ○ Yep ○ Nope

8. Ever been sent to the principal's office? ☐ Yep ☐ Nope

9. Most beautiful (inside) person you know? . . . .

10. How do you relax? . . . .

11. ○ Social butterfly ○ Wallflower?

12. Your biggest question about life? . . . .

13. ☐ Secret keeper ☐ Blabbermouth?

14. What makes you cry? . . . .

15. Names of future children? Boy . . . . Girl . . . .

16. Who's your favorite relative? . . . .

17. What was your last dream? . . . .

18. What makes you crazy? . . . .

19. I wish I . . . .

20. ○ Stick shift ○ Automatic ○ Can't drive yet?

21. Which appointment is worse? ☐ Doctor ☐ Dentist

22. Ever been to the emergency room? ◯ Yes ◯ No

23. ☐ Worry wart ☐ Worry free?

24. ◯ Bicycle through Europe ◯ African safari?

25. Favorite food court place? . . . .

26. ☐ Ice cubes ☐ Crushed ice?

27. What do you like on your burger? . . . .

28. Favorite fast food? . . . .

29. Favorite color of eyes? . . . .

30. Do you know sign language? ◯ YES ◯ NO

31. Favorite department store? . . . .

32. Who taught you to ride a bike? . . . .

33. How old were you when you learned to swim? . . . .

34. I would love to try . . . .

35. Who do you admire most? . . . .

36. ☐ Bikini ☐ Board shorts?

37. Worst movie ever? . . . .

38. Favorite kind of cookie? . . . .

39. Best commercial? . . . .

40. A word or phrase you say a lot? . . . .

1. FIRST, MIDDLE, AND LAST NAME? _ _ _ _ _ _ _ _ _ _ _ _ _

2. I CAN'T LIVE WITHOUT _ _ _ _ _ _ _ _ _ _ _ _ _ _ _ _ _ _

3. DO YOU TAKE VITAMINS? ☐ uh, yeah ☐ um, no

4. DO YOU FLOSS? ☐ uh, yeah ☐ um, no

5. HOW MANY HAIR PRODUCTS DO YOU USE? ☐ 1 ☐ 2 ☐ 3 ☐ ?

6. MEANEST THING YOU EVER DID TO A SIBLING? _ _ _ _ _ _ _ _

7. BELIEVE IN UFOs? ☐ uh, yeah ☐ um, no

8. CAN YOU IDENTIFY CONSTELLATIONS? ☐ uh, yeah ☐ um, no

9. ☐ CREAMY ☐ CRUNCHY PEANUT BUTTER?

10. SOMEONE YOU MISS? _ _ _ _ _ _ _ _ _ _ _ _ _ _ _ _ _ _

11. BELIEVE IN THE LOCH NESS MONSTER? ☐ uh, yeah ☐ um, no

12. BELIEVE IN BIG FOOT? ☐ uh, yeah ☐ um, no

13. WHICH WOULD YOU PICK? ☐ EXTRA $50 A WEEK ☐ 3-DAY WEEKEND

14. ANY PETS? ☐ uh, yeah _ _ _ _ _ _ _ _ _ _ _ _ _ _ ☐ um, no
(kind)

15. IF YES TO #14, NAMES _ _ _ _ _ _ _ _ _ _ _ _ _ _ _ _ _

16. MUSEUM OF ☐ ART ☐ NATURAL HISTORY?

17. ☐ TRAIN ☐ PLANE ☐ AUTOMOBILE?

18. I WISH MY HAIR _ _ _ _ _ _ _ _ _ _ _ _ _ _ _ _ _ _ _

19. BEST AMUSEMENT PARK RIDE? _ _ _ _ _ _ _ _ _ _ _ _ _ _

20. BEST LITTLE KID MOVIE? _ _ _ _ _ _ _ _ _ _ _ _ _ _ _

It's all about the fun time WOOf ?

BELIEVE IN YOUR FRIENDS

21. FAVORITE PICTURE BOOK? _ _ _ _ _ _ _ _ _ _ _ _ _ _ _ _ _ _

22. ☐ APPLES ☐ ORANGES?

23. ☐ CHOCOLATE MILK ☐ SOY MILK ☐ RICE MILK?

24. ☐ HOT DOG ☐ HAMBURGER?

25. I WISH SOMEONE WOULD INVENT _ _ _ _ _ _ _ _ _ _ _ _ _ _

26. ☐ WHITE ☐ WHEAT?

27. BEST ERA FOR FASHION? ☐ '60S ☐ '70S ☐ '80S ☐ '90S ☐ NOW

28. HOW MANY HOURS PER DAY ONLINE? _ _ _ _ _ _ _ _ _ _ _ _

29. HOW MANY HOURS PER DAY ON PHONE? _ _ _ _ _ _ _ _ _ _

30. JUST SAY NO TO _ _ _ _ _ _ _ _ _ _ _ _ _ _ _ _ _ _

31. ☐ FLIP-FLOPS ☐ STRAPPY SANDALS?

32. BEST FOOD COMES FROM WHICH COUNTRY? _ _ _ _ _ _ _ _

33. RUN AWAY FROM HOME WHEN YOU WERE LITTLE? ☐ UH, YEAH ☐ UM, NO

34. WHAT'S SCARIER? ☐ SNAKE ☐ SHARK

35. WHAT ARE YOU NOT GOOD AT? _ _ _ _ _ _ _ _ _ _ _ _ _ _ _

36. FRIEND YOU'VE HAD THE LONGEST? _ _ _ _ _ _ _ _ _ _ _ _ _

37. FRIEND WHO LIVES THE FARTHEST FROM YOU? _ _ _ _ _ _ _

38. WHERE DOES # 37 FRIEND LIVE? _ _ _ _ _ _ _ _ _ _ _ _ _

39. HOW MANY HOURS PER DAY WATCHING TV? _ _ _ _ _ _ _ _ _

40. WHICH ONE COULD YOU GIVE UP? ☐ E-MAIL ☐ CELL PHONE

yin

feet planted on the ground

c a l m

1. First, middle, and last name? _____

2. What toothpaste do you use? _____

3. ◯ Shop alone ◯ Shop with mom ◯ Shop with friends?

4. Best type of cake? _____

5. I love the smell of _____

6. How do you like your popcorn? _____

7. Favorite magazine? _____

8. ◯ Aspirin ◯ Aceteminifin ◯ Ibuprofen ◯ Tough it out?

9. What did you do last night? _____

10. ◯ Manicure ◯ Do-it-yourself nails?

11. What's your favorite comfort food? _____

12. ◯ High fashion ◯ Total casual?

13. ◯ Kill bugs ◯ Try to save them?

14. Best friend in kindergarten? _____

15. I can't bear the sound of _____

16. What was your favorite thing on the playground? _____

17. I would love to see _____

18. I would love to time-travel back to _____

19. I would love to time-travel forward to _____

20. Can you change a tire? ◯ Yes ◯ No

yang?
head in the clouds
c h a o s

21. Swallow anything by accident as a kid? ◯ Yes _____ (what) ◯ No

22. ◯ Romantic dinner for two ◯ Big party?

23. Favorite take-out food? _____

24. I can't stand the smell of _____

25. Favorite smoothie? _____

26. Ever tried dog or cat food? ◯ Yes ◯ No

27. Hair color? _____

28. 👀 ◯ Contacts ◯ Glasses ◯ Great vision?

29. Favorite game as a kid? _____

30. ◯ Salty ◯ Sweet?

31. I can't wait until I can _____

32. ◯ Lone Ranger ◯ Team player?

33. Do you try to find shapes in clouds? ◯ Yes ◯ No

34. ◯ Details ◯ Big picture?

35. What are you good at? _____

36. Favorite accessory? _____

37. ◯ Appointment for color ◯ Dye your own hair?

38. I love to listen to _____

39. Coolest thing you learned this week? _____

40. ◯ Tap ◯ Bottled ◯ Sparkling water?

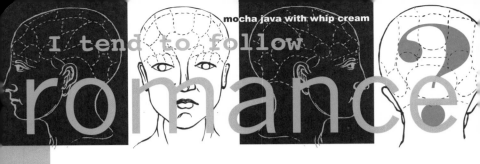

mocha java with whip cream

I tend to follow romance?

1. Name? _

2. ☐ Small talk ☐ Deep conversations?

3. ☐ Pilot ☐ Navigator?

4. Favorite ice cream flavor? _ _ _ _ _ _ _ _ _ _ _ _ _

5. I survived a ☐ hurricane ☐ tornado ☐ flood?

6. Favorite writer? _ _ _ _ _ _ _ _ _ _ _ _ _ _ _ _ _

7. Have you ever re-gifted? ☐ **YES** ☐ **NO**

8. ☐ Toilet-papered ☐ Toilet-paperer?

9. Favorite hot beverage? _ _ _ _ _ _ _ _ _ _ _ _ _

10. ☐ Time ☐ drags ☐ goes by too fast?

11. Most influential person in your life? _ _ _ _ _ _ _ _

12. Who would you be in a castle? ☐ Queen ☐ Princess ☐ Knight ☐ Jester

13. What do you daydream about? _ _ _ _ _ _ _ _ _ _

14. ☐ Meat eater ☐ Vegetarian ☐ Vegan?

15. Habit you wish you could change? _ _ _ _ _ _ _ _ _

16. Best type of movie? ☐ Romance ☐ Comedy ☐ Scary ☐ Action ☐ Sci-Fi

17. Any advice for a 5-year-old? _ _ _ _ _ _ _ _ _ _ _

18. ☐ Reality show ☐ Sitcom?

19. Birthday? _ _ _ _ _ _ _ _ _ _ _ _ _ _ _ _ _

20. ☐ Bagel ☐ Doughnut ☐ Croissant ☐ Cinnamon roll?

21. ☐ ☀ Morning glory ☐ 🌙 Night owl?

22. Favorite forest animal? _ _ _ _ _ _ _ _ _ _ _ _ _ _ _ _ _

23. Birthmark? ☐ **YES** ☐ **NO**

24. 🍬 Favorite candy? _ _ _ _ _ _ _ _ _ _

25. ☐ Store-bought ☐ Homemade?

26. I don't understand _ _ _ _ _ _ _ _ _ _ _

27. Who would you be on a set? ☐ Director ☐ Star ☐ Supporting star ☐ Set designer

28. What food/beverage do you get at the movies? _ _ _ _ _ _ _ _ _ _

29. Favorite color for a car? _ _ _ _ _ _ _ _ _ _ _

30. It's not fair that _ _ _ _ _ _ _ _ _ _ _ _ _ _

31. Do you make your bed every morning? ☐ **YES** ☐ **NO** 🛏

32. 🕶 Favorite costume you've ever worn? _ _ _ _ _ _ _ _

33. Are you always up-to-date on current news? ☐ **YES** ☐ **KIND OF** ☐ **NO**

34. ☐ Waffle cone ☐ Sugar cone ☐ Cup?

35. Which is worse? ☐ No TV ☐ No music

36. ☐ Small purse ☐ Giant bag?

37. Favorite fairy tale? _ _ _ _ _ _ _ _ _ _ _ _ _

38. Ever have an imaginary friend? ☐ **YES** _ _ _ _ _ _ _ _ ☐ **NO**
(Name)

39. Can different foods touch each other on your plate? ☐ **YES** ☐ **NO**

40. Best jungle animal? _ _ _ _ _ _ _ _ _ _ _

1. Name _____ Where were you born? _____

2. Sit ⭘ up front ⭘ in the back?

3. Favorite toy when you were a kid? _____

4. Which is worse? ⭘ Shopping for jeans ⭘ Shopping for bikini

5. Favorite season and why? _____

6. Do you read the ending before you finish a book? ⭘ Yes ⭘ No

7. Best brand of jeans? _____

8. ⭘ Island cabana ⭘ European castle ⭘ Safari tent ⭘ Ski lodge

9. Favorite color combination? _____

10. ⭘ Sunset ⭘ Sunrise?

11. Favorite number? _____ Why? _____

12. Color your toes are painted? _____

13. Ever needed stitches? ⭘ Yes Why? _____ ⭘ No

14. My favorite shoes are _____

15. ⭘ Right-handed ⭘ Left-handed ⭘ Ambidextrous?

16. How many children would you like someday? _____

17. ⭘ Tent ⭘ Cabin?

18. What scared you as a kid? _____

19. For just a day, I would switch places with _____

20. Wake up to ⭘ alarm ⭘ radio?

21. Been in a talent show? ◯ Yes Talent? _____ No ◯

22. ◯ Go with the flow   ◯ Stick to a routine?

23. Coolest first name? _____

24. ◯ Polka dots ◯ Stripes ◯ Plaid ◯ Paisley?

25. Coolest last name? _____

26. ◯ Paper ◯ Plastic?

27. What can you draw well? _____

28. ◯ Brownies ◯ Chocolate chip cookies

29. I will not eat _____

30. ◯ Gold ◯ Silver?

31. Favorite hangout? _____

32. How many times have you moved in your life? _____

33. As a kid, ◯ stuffed animal ◯ blankie?

34. Favorite thing to do on the weekend? _____

35. What color is your bedroom? _____

36. ◯ Mild ◯ Spicy?

37. What would be hard to give up? _____

38. Cutest thing your pet does? _____

39. ◯ Shower ◯ Bath?

40. I have a problem with _____

1. What is your full name? . . . .

2. Nickname? . . . .

3. ◯ Coke   ◯ Pepsi?

4. Favorite song? . . . .

5. Earliest memory? . . . .

6. ◯ Milk   ◯ Dark chocolate?

7. Who do you call when you're upset? . . . .

8. Do you recycle? ♻ ☐ yes ☐ no

9. ◯ Big Mac   ◯ Whopper?

10. Last book you read? . . . .

11. ◯ 🏖 Beach   ◯ 🏔 Mountains?

12. What kind of shoes are you wearing? . . . .

13. ◯ TV   ◯ Book?

14. Favorite store? . . . .

15. What was the last thing you ate? 🍜 . . . .

16. ◯ Clean freak   ◯ Total slob?

17. Favorite car? . . . .

18. Best gift you've ever received? . . . .

19. Best gift you've ever given? . . . .

20. Do you wish on ★ ★ ★ ? yes ☐ no ☐

21. Ever been stung by a jellyfish? ☐ yes ☐ no

22. Best cartoon ever? . . . .

23. What scares you? . . . .

24. Last person you spoke to? . . . .

25. Favorite doughnut? . . . .

26. Stupidest thing you've ever done? . . . .

27. Been to NYC? ☐ yes ☐ no

28. Best sitcom ever? . . . .

29. Been to LA? ☐ yes ☐ no

30. Favorite place you've visited? . . . .

31. Least favorite vegetable? . . . .

32. ○ Dreamer ○ Doer?

33. One word to describe you? . . . .

34. Name of your very first friend? . . . .

35. If I could, I would change my first name to . . . .

36. ○ Night light ○ Completely dark?

37. Ever pull an all-nighter? . . . .

38. Believe in love at first sight? ☐ yes ☐ no

39. Best toppings for pizza? . . . .

40. Ever owned a goldfish? ☐ yes name . . . . ☐ no

coke-or-pepsi.com

1. Name given at birth? _____

2. What do your friends call you? _____

3. What do you do when you're mad? _____

4. Favorite holiday and why? _____

5. Ever won anything? ☐ *yeah* What? _____ ☐ *nah*

6. What do you do on rainy days? ☂ _____

7. 🐕 ◯ 🐈 ◯ person?

8. Favorite flower? _____

9. ◯ Coffee ◯ Tea?

10. Oldest living relative: 👤 Name _____ Age _____

11. Most annoying bug? _____

12. ◯ Tanning oil ◯ Sunscreen?

13. Nails: ◯ Painted ◯ Chipped ◯ Fake ◯ Bitten?

14. Wear painful shoes just because they're cute? ☐ *yeah* ☐ *nah*

15. Best type of music? _____

16. Ever been in love? ☐ *yeah* ☐ *nah*

17. Favorite actor? _____

18. ◯ Radio ◯ iPod?

19. Favorite actress? _____

20. Do you have a secret you've never told anyone? ☐ *yeah* ☐ *nah*

21. Did you ever believe in the Tooth Fairy? ☐ yeah ☐ nah

22. Favorite thing to nosh on? _____

23. ◯ Mall ◯ Outlet

24. Your absolute favorite article of clothing? _____

25. ◯ Frozen yogurt ◯ Ice cream?

26. What superpower would you love to have? _____

27. ◯ Potato chips ◯ French fries?

28. Cosmetic you can't live without? _____

29. Best teacher you ever had? _____

30. ◯ Spender ◯ Saver?

31. Who should play you in a movie version of your life? _____

32. If you were an animal, what would you be? _____

33. Best beverage? _____

34. Favorite cereal? _____

35. Who do you wish you could meet? _____

36. ◯ Fearful ◯ Fearless?

37. Which would you try? ◯ Skydiving ◯ Rappelling ◯ Scuba Diving

38. ◯ Butterflies ◯ Dragonflies?

39. ◯ Organic ◯ Junk food?

40. Favorite school subject? _____

1. What's your full name? . . . .

2. Elementary school: ☐ Bully ☐ Bullied?

3. Dream job? . . . .

4. Glass: ○ ½ full ○ ½ empty?

5. Ever broken a body part? ☐ Yep What? . . . . ☐ Nope

6. How many car accidents have you been in? . . . .

7. Ever caused a car accident? ○ Yep ○ Nope

8. 😠 Ever been sent to the principal's office? ☐ Yep ☐ Nope

9. Most beautiful (inside) person you know? . . . .

10. How do you relax? . . . .

11. ○ Social butterfly 🦋 ○ Wallflower? 🌼

12. Your biggest question about life? . . . .

13. ☐ Secret keeper ☐ Blabbermouth?

14. What makes you cry? . . . .

15. 👶 Names of future children? Boy . . . . Girl . . . .

16. Who's your favorite relative? . . . .

17. 🌙 What was your last dream? . . . .

18. What makes you crazy? 😖 . . . .

19. I wish I . . . .

20. ○ Stick shift ○ Automatic ○ Can't drive yet?

21. Which appointment is worse? ☐ Doctor ☐ Dentist

22. Ever been to the emergency room? ◯ Yes ◯ No

23. ☐ Worry wart ☐ Worry free?

24. ◯ Bicycle through Europe ◯ African safari?

25. Favorite food court place? . . . .

26. ☐ Ice cubes ☐ Crushed ice?

27. 🥣 What do you like on your burger? . . . .

28. Favorite fast food? . . . .

29. Favorite color of eyes? . . . .

30. Do you know sign language? ◯ YES ◯ NO

31. Favorite department store? . . . .

32. Who taught you to ride a bike? 🚲 . . . .

33. How old were you when you learned to swim? . . . .

34. I would love to try . . . .

35. Who do you admire most? . . . .

36. ☐ Bikini ☐ Board shorts?

37. Worst movie ever? . . . .

38. Favorite kind of cookie? . . . .

39. Best commercial? 📺 . . . .

40. A word or phrase you say a lot? . . . .

1. First, middle, and last name? _ _ _ _ _ _ _ _ _ _ _ _ _ _ _ _

2. I can't live without _

3. Do you take vitamins? ☐ uh, yeah ☐ um, no

4. Do you floss? ☐ uh, yeah ☐ um, no

5. How many hair products do you use? ☐ 1 ☐ 2 ☐ 3 ☐ ?

6. Meanest thing you ever did to a sibling? _ _ _ _ _ _ _ _ _ _

7. Believe in UFOs? ☐ uh, yeah ☐ um, no

8. Can you identify constellations? ☐ uh, yeah ☐ um, no

9. ☐ Creamy ☐ Crunchy Peanut Butter?

10. Someone you miss? _ _ _ _ _ _ _ _ _ _ _ _ _ _ _ _ _ _ _

11. Believe in the Loch Ness Monster? ☐ uh, yeah ☐ um, no

12. Believe in Big Foot? ☐ uh, yeah ☐ um, no

13. Which would you pick? ☐ Extra $50 a week ☐ 3-day weekend

14. Any pets? ☐ uh, yeah _ _ _ _ _ _ _ _ _ _ _ _ ☐ um, no
     (kind)

15. If yes to #14, Names _ _ _ _ _ _ _ _ _ _ _ _ _ _ _ _ _ _ _

16. Museum of ☐ art ☐ natural history?

17. ☐ Train ☐ Plane ☐ Automobile?

18. I wish my hair _

19. Best amusement park ride? _ _ _ _ _ _ _ _ _ _ _ _ _ _

20. Best little kid movie? _ _ _ _ _ _ _ _ _ _ _ _ _ _ _ _ _

21. FAVORITE PICTURE BOOK? _ _ _ _ _ _ _ _

22. ☐ APPLES ☐ ORANGES?

23. ☐ CHOCOLATE MILK ☐ SOY MILK ☐ RICE MILK?

24. ☐ HOT DOG ☐ HAMBURGER?

25. I WISH SOMEONE WOULD INVENT _ _ _ _ _ _ _ _ _

26. ☐ WHITE ☐ WHEAT?

27. BEST ERA FOR FASHION? ☐ '60s ☐ '70s ☐ '80s ☐ '90s ☐ NOW

28. HOW MANY HOURS PER DAY ONLINE? _ _ _ _ _ _

29. HOW MANY HOURS PER DAY ON PHONE? _ _ _ _ _ _

30. JUST SAY NO TO _ _ _ _ _ _ _ _ _

31. ☐ FLIP-FLOPS ☐ STRAPPY SANDALS?

32. BEST FOOD COMES FROM WHICH COUNTRY? _ _ _ _

33. RUN AWAY FROM HOME WHEN YOU WERE LITTLE? ☐ UH, YEAH ☐ UM, NO

34. WHAT'S SCARIER? ☐ SNAKE ☐ SHARK

35. WHAT ARE YOU NOT GOOD AT? _ _ _ _ _ _ _

36. FRIEND YOU'VE HAD THE LONGEST? _ _ _ _ _ _

37. FRIEND WHO LIVES THE FARTHEST FROM YOU? _ _ _ _

38. WHERE DOES # 37 FRIEND LIVE? _ _ _ _ _ _

39. HOW MANY HOURS PER DAY WATCHING TV? _ _ _ _

40. WHICH ONE COULD YOU GIVE UP? ☐ E-MAIL ☐ CELL PHONE

1. First, middle, and last name? _____

2. What toothpaste do you use? _____

3. ◯ Shop alone ◯ Shop with mom ◯ Shop with friends?

4. Best type of cake? _____

5. I love the smell of _____

6. How do you like your popcorn? _____

7. Favorite magazine? _____

8. ◯ Aspirin ◯ Aceteminifin ◯ Ibuprofen ◯ Tough it out?

9. What did you do last night? _____

10. ◯ Manicure ◯ Do-it-yourself nails?

11. What's your favorite comfort food? _____

12. ◯ High fashion ◯ Total casual?

13. ◯ Kill bugs ◯ Try to save them?

14. Best friend in kindergarten? _____

15. I can't bear the sound of _____

16. What was your favorite thing on the playground?_____

17. I would love to see _____

18. I would love to time-travel back to _____

19. I would love to time-travel forward to _____

20. Can you change a tire? ◯ Yes ◯ No

yang?
head in the clouds
c h a o s

21. Swallow anything by accident as a kid? ◯ Yes _____ ◯ No
(what)

22. ◯ Romantic dinner for two ◯ Big party?

23. Favorite take-out food? _____

24. I can't stand the smell of _____

25. Favorite smoothie? _____

26. Ever tried dog or cat food? ◯ Yes ◯ No

27. Hair color? _____

28. 👀 ◯ Contacts ◯ Glasses ◯ Great vision?

29. Favorite game as a kid? _____

30. ◯ Salty ◯ Sweet?

31. I can't wait until I can _____

32. ◯ Lone Ranger ◯ Team player?

33. Do you try to find shapes in clouds? ◯ Yes ◯ No

34. ◯ Details ◯ Big picture?

35. What are you good at? _____

36. Favorite accessory? _____

37. ◯ Appointment for color ◯ Dye your own hair?

38. I love to listen to _____

39. Coolest thing you learned this week? _____

40. ◯ Tap ◯ Bottled ◯ Sparkling water?

coke-or-pepsi.com

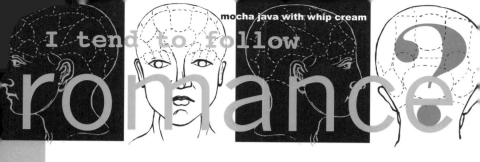

1. Name? _

2. ☐ Small talk ☐ Deep conversations?

3. ☐ Pilot ☐ Navigator?

4. Favorite ice cream flavor? _ _ _ _ _ _ _ _ _ _ _ _ _

5. I survived a ☐ hurricane ☐ tornado ☐ flood?

6. Favorite writer? _ _ _ _ _ _ _ _ _ _ _ _ _ _ _ _ _

7. Have you ever re-gifted? ☐ **YES** ☐ **NO**

8. ☐ Toilet-papered ☐ Toilet-paperer?

9. Favorite hot beverage? _ _ _ _ _ _ _ _ _ _ _ _

10. ⏰ Time ☐ drags ☐ goes by too fast?

11. Most influential person in your life? _ _ _ _ _ _ _ _ _ _ _

12. Who would you be in a castle? ☐ Queen ☐ Princess ☐ Knight ☐ Jester

13. What do you daydream about? ☺ _ _ _ _ _ _ _ _ _ _ _ _ _

14. ☐ Meat eater ☐ Vegetarian ☐ Vegan?

15. Habit you wish you could change? _ _ _ _ _ _ _ _ _ _ _

16. Best type of movie? ☐ Romance ☐ Comedy ☐ Scary ☐ Action ☐ Sci-Fi

17. Any advice for a 5-year-old? _ _ _ _ _ _ _ _ _ _ _

18. ☐ Reality show ☐ Sitcom?

19. Birthday? _ _ _ _ _ _ _ _ _ _ _ _ _ _ _ _

20. ☐ Bagel ☐ Doughnut ☐ Croissant ☐ Cinnamon roll?

21. ☐ ☀ Morning glory ☐ 🌙 Night owl?

22. Favorite forest animal? _ _ _ _ _ _ _ _ _ _ _ _ _ _

23. Birthmark? ☐ **YES** ☐ **NO**

24. 🍬 Favorite candy? _ _ _ _ _ _ _ _ _ _ _ _ _ _

25. ☐ Store-bought ☐ Homemade?

26. I don't understand _ _ _ _ _ _ _ _ _ _ _ _ _ _

27. Who would you be on a set? ☐ Director ☐ Star ☐ Supporting star ☐ Set designer

28. What food/beverage do you get at the movies? _ _ _ _ _ _ _ _

29. Favorite color for a car? _ _ _ _ _ _ _ _ _ _ _

30. It's not fair that _ _ _ _ _ _ _ _ _ _ _ _ _ _

31. Do you make your bed every morning? ☐ **YES** ☐ **NO** 🛏

32. 🕶 Favorite costume you've ever worn? _ _ _ _ _ _ _

33. Are you always up-to-date on current news? ☐ **YES** ☐ **KIND OF** ☐ **NO**

34. ☐ Waffle cone ☐ Sugar cone ☐ Cup?

35. Which is worse? ☐ No TV ☐ No music

36. ☐ Small purse ☐ Giant bag?

37. Favorite fairy tale? _ _ _ _ _ _ _ _ _ _ _ _

38. Ever have an imaginary friend? ☐ **YES** _ _ _ _ _ _ _ ☐ **NO**
                                              (Name)

39. Can different foods touch each other on your plate? ☐ **YES** ☐ **NO**

🐒 40. Best jungle animal? _ _ _ _ _ _ _ _ _ _ _ _

1. Name _____Where were you born? _____

2. Sit ◯ up front   ◯ in the back?

3. Favorite toy when you were a kid? _____

4. Which is worse? ◯ Shopping for jeans   ◯ Shopping for bikini

5. Favorite season and why? _____

6. Do you read the ending before you finish a book? ◯ Yes   ◯ No

7. Best brand of jeans? _____

8. ◯ Island cabana ◯ European castle ◯ Safari tent ◯ Ski lodge

9. Favorite color combination? _____

10. ◯ Sunset   ◯ Sunrise?

11. Favorite number? _____ Why? _____

12. Color your toes are painted? _____

13. Ever needed stitches? ◯ Yes Why? _____ ◯ No

14. My favorite shoes are _____

15. ◯ Right-handed   ◯ Left-handed   ◯ Ambidextrous?

16. How many children would you like someday? _____

17. ◯ Tent   ◯ Cabin?

18. What scared you as a kid? _____

19. For just a day, I would switch places with _____

20. Wake up to ◯ alarm   ◯ radio?

fire roasted with jalapeños

spicy

soak up the sun

21. Been in a talent show? ◯ Yes Talent? _____ No ◯

22. ◯ Go with the flow   ◯ Stick to a routine?

23. Coolest first name? _____

24. ◯ Polka dots   ◯ Stripes   ◯ Plaid   ◯ Paisley?

25. Coolest last name? _____

26. ◯ Paper   ◯ Plastic?

27. What can you draw well? _____

28. ◯ Brownies   ◯ Chocolate chip cookies

29. I will not eat _____

30. ◯ Gold   ◯ Silver?

31. Favorite hangout? _____

32. How many times have you moved in your life? _____

33. As a kid, ◯ stuffed animal   ◯ blankie?

34. Favorite thing to do on the weekend? _____

35. What color is your bedroom? _____

36. ◯ Mild   ◯ Spicy?

37. What would be hard to give up? _____

38. Cutest thing your pet does? _____

39. ◯ Shower   ◯ Bath?

40. I have a problem with _____

bittersweet

secret

my room is a total mess

1. What is your full name? . . . .

2. Nickname? . . . .

3. ◯ Coke ◯ Pepsi?

4. Favorite song? . . . .

5. Earliest memory? . . . .

6. ◯ Milk ◯ Dark chocolate?

7. Who do you call when you're upset? . . . .

8. Do you recycle? ♲ ☐ yes ☐ no

9. ◯ Big Mac ◯ Whopper?

10. Last book you read? . . . .

11. ◯ 🏖 Beach ◯ ⛰ Mountains?

12. What kind of shoes are you wearing? . . . .

13. ◯ TV ◯ Book?

14. Favorite store? . . . .

15. What was the last thing you ate? 🥢 . . . .

16. ◯ Clean freak ◯ Total slob?

17. Favorite car? . . . .

18. Best gift you've ever received? . . . .

19. Best gift you've ever given? . . . .

20. Do you wish on ★ ★ ★ ? yes ☐ no ☐

21. Ever been stung by a jellyfish? ☐ yes ☐ no

22. Best cartoon ever? . . . .

23. What scares you? . . . .

24. Last person you spoke to? . . . .

25. Favorite doughnut? . . . .

26. Stupidest thing you've ever done? . . . .

27. Been to NYC? ☐ yes ☐ no

28. Best sitcom ever? . . . .

29. Been to LA? ☐ yes ☐ no

30. Favorite place you've visited? . . . .

31. Least favorite vegetable? . . . .

32. ◯ Dreamer ◯ Doer?

33. One word to describe you? . . . .

34. Name of your very first friend? . . . .

35. If I could, I would change my first name to . . . .

36. ◯ Night light ◯ Completely dark?

37. Ever pull an all-nighter? . . . .

38. Believe in love at first sight? ☐ yes ☐ no

39. Best toppings for pizza? . . . .

40. Ever owned a goldfish? ☐ yes name . . . . ☐ no

coke-or-pepsi.com

I am always in the know

crazy

with cheese

1. Name given at birth? _____

2. What do your friends call you? _____

3. What do you do when you're mad? _____

4. Favorite holiday and why? _____

5. Ever won anything? ☐ yeah What? _____ ☐ nah

6. What do you do on rainy days? ☂ _____

7. 🐕 ◯   🐈 ◯ person?

8. Favorite flower? _____

9. ◯ Coffee ◯ Tea?

10. Oldest living relative: 👴 Name _____ Age _____

11. Most annoying bug? _____

12. ◯ Tanning oil ◯ Sunscreen?

13. Nails: ◯ Painted ◯ Chipped ◯ Fake ◯ Bitten?

14. Wear painful shoes just because they're cute? ☐ yeah ☐ nah

15. Best type of music? _____

16. Ever been in love? ☐ yeah ☐ nah

17. Favorite actor? _____

18. ◯ Radio ◯ iPod?

19. Favorite actress? _____

20. Do you have a secret you've never told anyone? ☐ yeah ☐ nah

21. Did you ever believe in the Tooth Fairy? ☐ yeah ☐ nah

22. 🍕 Favorite thing to nosh on? _____

23. ◯ Mall ◯ Outlet

24. 🎀 Your absolute favorite article of clothing? _____

25. ◯ Frozen yogurt ◯ Ice cream?

26. What superpower would you love to have? _____

27. ◯ Potato chips ◯ French fries?

28. Cosmetic you can't live without? 💄 _____

29. Best teacher you ever had? _____

30. ◯ Spender ◯ Saver?

31. Who should play you in a movie version of your life? _____

32. If you were an animal, what would you be? _____

33. 🥫 Best beverage? _____

34. Favorite cereal? _____

35. Who do you wish you could meet? _____

36. 😨 ◯ Fearful 😄 ◯ Fearless?

37. Which would you try? ◯ Skydiving ◯ Rappelling ◯ Scuba Diving

38. ◯ Butterflies ◯ Dragonflies?

39. 🫛 ◯ Organic ◯ Junk food? 🍬

40. Favorite school subject? _____

1. What's your full name? . . . .

2. Elementary school: ☐ Bully   ☐ Bullied?

3. Dream job? . . . .

4. Glass: ○ ½ full   ○ ½ empty?

5. Ever broken a body part? ☐ Yep What? . . . . ☐ Nope

6. How many car accidents have you been in? . . . .

7. Ever caused a car accident? ○ Yep ○ Nope

8. 😠 Ever been sent to the principal's office? ☐ Yep ☐ Nope

9. Most beautiful (inside) person you know? . . . .

10. How do you relax? . . . .

11. ○ Social butterfly 🦋   ○ Wallflower? 🌼

12. Your biggest question about life? . . . .

13. ☐ Secret keeper   ☐ Blabbermouth?

14. What makes you cry? . . . .

15. 👶 Names of future children? Boy . . . . Girl . . . .

16. Who's your favorite relative? . . . .

17. 🌙 What was your last dream? . . . .

18. What makes you crazy? 😖 . . . .

19. I wish I . . . .

20. ○ Stick shift ○ Automatic ○ Can't drive yet?

21. Which appointment is worse? ☐ Doctor ☐ Dentist

22. Ever been to the emergency room? ◯ Yes ◯ No

23. ☐ Worry wart ☐ Worry free?

24. ◯ Bicycle through Europe ◯ African safari?

25. Favorite food court place? . . . .

26. ☐ Ice cubes ☐ Crushed ice?

27. 🍔 What do you like on your burger? . . . .

28. Favorite fast food? . . . .

29. Favorite color of eyes? . . . .

30. Do you know sign language? ◯ YES ◯ NO

31. Favorite department store? . . . .

32. Who taught you to ride a bike? 🚲 . . . .

33. How old were you when you learned to swim? . . . .

34. I would love to try . . . .

35. Who do you admire most? . . . .

36. ☐ Bikini ☐ Board shorts?

37. Worst movie ever? . . . .

38. Favorite kind of cookie? . . . .

39. Best commercial? 📺 . . . .

40. A word or phrase you say a lot? . . . .

1. First, middle, and last name? _ _ _ _ _ _ _ _ _ _ _ _ _ _ _ _ _

2. I can't live without _ .

3. Do you take vitamins? ☐ uh, yeah ☐ um, no

4. Do you floss? ☐ uh, yeah ☐ um, no

5. How many hair products do you use? ☐ 1 ☐ 2 ☐ 3 ☐ ?

6. Meanest thing you ever did to a sibling? _ _ _ _ _ _ _ _ _ .

7. Believe in UFOs? ☐ uh, yeah ☐ um, no

8. Can you identify constellations? ☐ uh, yeah ☐ um, no

9. ☐ Creamy ☐ Crunchy Peanut Butter?

10. Someone you miss? _ _ _ _ _ _ _ _ _ _ _ _ _ _ _ _ _ _

11. Believe in the Loch Ness Monster? ☐ uh, yeah ☐ um, no

12. Believe in Big Foot? ☐ uh, yeah ☐ um, no

13. Which would you pick? ☐ Extra $50 a week ☐ 3-day weekend

14. Any pets? ☐ uh, yeah _ _ _ _ _ _ _ _ _ _ _ ☐ um, no
                                    (kind)

15. If yes to #14, names _ _ _ _ _ _ _ _ _ _ _ _ _ _ _ _ _

16. Museum of ☐ art ☐ natural history?

17. ☐ Train ☐ Plane ☐ Automobile?

18. I wish my hair _ _ _ _ _ _ _ _ _ _ _ _ _ _ _ _ _ _

19. Best amusement park ride? _ _ _ _ _ _ _ _ _ _ _ _ _ _

20. Best little kid movie? _ _ _ _ _ _ _ _ _ _ _ _ _ _ _

21. Favorite picture book? _ _ _ _ _ _ _ _ _ _ _ _ _ _ _

22. ☐ Apples ☐ Oranges?

23. ☐ Chocolate milk ☐ Soy milk ☐ Rice milk?

24. ☐ Hot dog ☐ Hamburger?

25. I wish someone would invent _ _ _ _ _ _ _ _ _ _ _ _ _

26. ☐ White ☐ wheat?

27. Best era for fashion? ☐ '60s ☐ '70s ☐ '80s ☐ '90s ☐ now

28. How many hours per day online? _ _ _ _ _ _ _ _ _

29. How many hours per day on phone? _ _ _ _ _ _ _ _

30. Just say no to _ _ _ _ _ _ _ _ _ _ _ _ _ _ _ _

31. ☐ Flip-flops ☐ Strappy sandals?

32. Best food comes from which country? _ _ _ _ _ _ _

33. Run away from home when you were little? ☐ uh, yeah ☐ um, no

34. What's scarier? ☐ Snake ☐ Shark

35. What are you not good at? _ _ _ _ _ _ _ _ _ _

36. Friend you've had the longest? _ _ _ _ _ _ _ _ _

37. Friend who lives the farthest from you? _ _ _ _ _ _

38. Where does # 37 friend live? _ _ _ _ _ _ _ _ _

39. How many hours per day watching TV? _ _ _ _ _ _

40. Which one could you give up? ☐ E-mail ☐ Cell phone

? yin
feet planted on the ground
c a l m

1. First, middle, and last name? _____

2. What toothpaste do you use? _____

3. ⬡ Shop alone ⬡ Shop with mom ⬡ Shop with friends?

4. Best type of cake? _____

5. I love the smell of _____

6. How do you like your popcorn? _____

7. Favorite magazine? _____

8. ⬡ Aspirin ⬡ Aceteminifin ⬡ Ibuprofen ⬡ Tough it out?

9. What did you do last night? _____

10. ⬡ Manicure ⬡ Do-it-yourself nails?

11. What's your favorite comfort food? _____

12. ⬡ High fashion ⬡ Total casual?

13. ⬡ Kill bugs ⬡ Try to save them?

14. Best friend in kindergarten? _____

15. I can't bear the sound of _____

16. What was your favorite thing on the playground? _____

17. I would love to see _____

18. I would love to time-travel back to _____

19. I would love to time-travel forward to _____

20. Can you change a tire? ⬡ Yes ⬡ No

21. Swallow anything by accident as a kid? ◯ Yes _____ ◯ No
      (what)

22. ◯ Romantic dinner for two ◯ Big party?

23. Favorite take-out food? _____

24. I can't stand the smell of _____

25. Favorite smoothie? _____

26. Ever tried dog or cat food? ◯ Yes ◯ No

27. Hair color? _____

28. 👁 👁 ◯ Contacts ◯ Glasses ◯ Great vision?

29. Favorite game as a kid? _____

30. ◯ Salty ◯ Sweet?

31. I can't wait until I can _____

32. ◯ Lone Ranger ◯ Team player?

33. Do you try to find shapes in clouds? ◯ Yes ◯ No

34. ◯ Details ◯ Big picture?

35. What are you good at? _____

36. Favorite accessory? _____

37. ◯ Appointment for color ◯ Dye your own hair?

38. I love to listen to _____

39. Coolest thing you learned this week? _____

40. ◯ Tap ◯ Bottled ◯ Sparkling water?

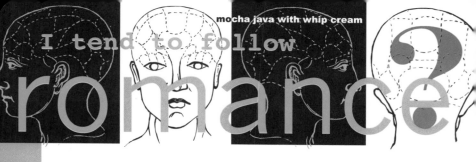

mocha java with whip cream

I tend to follow romance?

1. Name? _

2. ☐ Small talk ☐ Deep conversations?

3. ☐ Pilot ☐ Navigator?

4. Favorite ice cream flavor? _ _ _ _ _ _ _ _ _ _ _ _ _ _ _

5. I survived a ☐ hurricane ☐ tornado ☐ flood?

6. Favorite writer? _ _ _ _ _ _ _ _ _ _ _ _ _ _ _

7. Have you ever re-gifted? ☐ YES ☐ NO

8. ☐ Toilet-papered ☐ Toilet-paperer?

9. Favorite hot beverage? _ _ _ _ _ _ _ _ _ _ _ _ _ _ _

10. Time ☐ drags ☐ goes by too fast?

11. Most influential person in your life? _ _ _ _ _ _ _ _ _

12. Who would you be in a castle? ☐ Queen ☐ Princess ☐ Knight ☐ Jester

13. What do you daydream about? _ _ _ _ _ _ _ _ _ _ _ _

14. ☐ Meat eater ☐ Vegetarian ☐ Vegan?

15. Habit you wish you could change? _ _ _ _ _ _ _ _ _ _

16. Best type of movie? ☐ Romance ☐ Comedy ☐ Scary ☐ Action ☐ Sci-Fi

17. Any advice for a 5-year-old? _ _ _ _ _ _ _ _ _ _ _ _

18. ☐ Reality show ☐ Sitcom?

19. Birthday? _ _ _ _ _ _ _ _ _ _ _

20. ☐ Bagel ☐ Doughnut ☐ Croissant ☐ Cinnamon roll?

21. ☐ ☀ Morning glory ☐ ☾ Night owl?

22. Favorite forest animal? _ _ _ _ _ _ _ _ _ _ _ _ _

23. Birthmark? ☐ **YES** ☐ **NO**

24. 🍬 Favorite candy? _ _ _ _ _ _ _ _ _ _ _ _ _

25. ☐ Store-bought ☐ Homemade?

26. I don't understand _ _ _ _ _ _ _ _ _ _ _ _ _ _ _ _ _

27. Who would you be on a set? ☐ Director ☐ Star ☐ Supporting star ☐ Set designer

28. What food/beverage do you get at the movies?_ _ _ _ _ _ _ _ _

29. Favorite color for a car? _ _ _ _ _ _ _ _ _ _ _ _

30. It's not fair that _ _ _ _ _ _ _ _ _ _ _ _ _ _ _

31. Do you make your bed every morning? ☐ **YES** ☐ **NO** 🛏

32. 🖌 Favorite costume you've ever worn? _ _ _ _ _ _ _ _

33. Are you always up-to-date on current news? ☐ **YES** ☐ **KIND OF** ☐ **NO**

34. ☐ Waffle cone ☐ Sugar cone ☐ Cup?

35. Which is worse? ☐ No TV ☐ No music

36. ☐ Small purse ☐ Giant bag?

37. Favorite fairy tale? _ _ _ _ _ _ _ _ _ _ _ _ _ _ _

38. Ever have an imaginary friend? ☐ **YES** _ _ _ _ _ _ _ _ _ _ ☐ **NO**
(Name)

39. Can different foods touch each other on your plate? ☐ **YES** ☐ **NO**

🐒 40. Best jungle animal?_ _ _ _ _ _ _ _ _ _ _ _ _ _ _

1. Name _____ Where were you born? _____

2. Sit ◯ up front ◯ in the back?

3. Favorite toy when you were a kid? _____

4. Which is worse? ◯ Shopping for jeans ◯ Shopping for bikini

5. Favorite season and why? _____

6. Do you read the ending before you finish a book? ◯ Yes ◯ No

7. Best brand of jeans? _____

8. ◯ Island cabana ◯ European castle ◯ Safari tent ◯ Ski lodge

9. Favorite color combination? _____

10. ◯ Sunset ◯ Sunrise?

11. Favorite number? _____ Why? _____

12. Color your toes are painted? _____

13. Ever needed stitches? ◯ Yes Why? _____ ◯ No

14. My favorite shoes are _____

15. ◯ Right-handed ◯ Left-handed ◯ Ambidextrous?

16. How many children would you like someday? _____

17. ◯ Tent ◯ Cabin?

18. What scared you as a kid? _____

19. For just a day, I would switch places with _____

20. Wake up to ◯ alarm ◯ radio?

21. Been in a talent show? ◯ Yes Talent? _____ No ◯

22. ◯ Go with the flow   ◯ Stick to a routine?

23. Coolest first name? _____

24. ◯ Polka dots ◯ Stripes ◯ Plaid ◯ Paisley?

25. Coolest last name? _____

26. ◯ Paper ◯ Plastic?

27. What can you draw well? _____

28. ◯ Brownies ◯ Chocolate chip cookies

29. I will not eat _____

30. ◯ Gold ◯ Silver?

31. Favorite hangout? _____

32. How many times have you moved in your life? _____

33. As a kid, ◯ stuffed animal ◯ blankie?

34. Favorite thing to do on the weekend? _____

35. What color is your bedroom? _____

36. ◯ Mild ◯ Spicy?

37. What would be hard to give up? _____

38. Cutest thing your pet does? _____

39. ◯ Shower ◯ Bath?

40. I have a problem with _____

1. What is your full name? ....

2. Nickname? ....

3. ◯ Coke ◯ Pepsi?

4. Favorite song? ....

5. Earliest memory? ....

6. ◯ Milk ◯ Dark chocolate?

7. Who do you call when you're upset? ....

8. Do you recycle? ♻ ☐ yes ☐ no

9. ◯ Big Mac ◯ Whopper?

10. Last book you read? ....

11. ◯ 🏖 Beach ◯ 🏔 Mountains?

12. What kind of shoes are you wearing? ....

13. ◯ TV ◯ Book?

14. Favorite store? ....

15. What was the last thing you ate? 🥢🍜 ....

16. ◯ Clean freak ◯ Total slob?

17. Favorite car? ....

18. Best gift you've ever received? ....

19. Best gift you've ever given? ....

20. Do you wish on ★★★? yes ☐ no ☐

21. Ever been stung by a jellyfish? ☐ yes ☐ no

22. Best cartoon ever? . . . .

23. What scares you? . . . .

24. Last person you spoke to? . . . .

25. Favorite doughnut? . . . .

26. Stupidest thing you've ever done? . . . .

27. Been to NYC? ☐ yes ☐ no

28. Best sitcom ever? . . . .

29. Been to LA? ☐ yes ☐ no

30. Favorite place you've visited? . . . .

31. Least favorite vegetable? . . . .

32. ◯ Dreamer ◯ Doer?

33. One word to describe you? . . . .

34. Name of your very first friend? . . . .

35. If I could, I would change my first name to . . . .

36. ◯ Night light ◯ Completely dark?

37. Ever pull an all-nighter? . . . .

38. Believe in love at first sight? ☐ yes ☐ no

39. Best toppings for pizza? . . . .

40. Ever owned a goldfish? ☐ yes name . . . . ☐ no

1. Name given at birth? _____

2. What do your friends call you? _____

3. What do you do when you're mad? _____

4. Favorite holiday and why? _____

5. Ever won anything? ☐ yeah What? _____ ☐ nah

6. What do you do on rainy days? ☂ _____

7. 🐆 ◯   🐈 ◯ person?

8. Favorite flower? _____

9. ◯ Coffee ◯ Tea?

10. Oldest living relative: 👵 Name _____ Age _____

11. Most annoying bug? _____

12. ◯ Tanning oil ◯ Sunscreen?

13. Nails: ◯ Painted ◯ Chipped ◯ Fake ◯ Bitten?

14. Wear painful shoes just because they're cute? ☐ yeah ☐ nah

15. Best type of music? _____

16. Ever been in love? ☐ yeah ☐ nah

17. Favorite actor? _____

18. ◯ Radio ◯ iPod?

19. Favorite actress? _____

20. Do you have a secret you've never told anyone? ☐ yeah ☐ nah

21. Did you ever believe in the Tooth Fairy? ☐ yeah ☐ nah

22. Favorite thing to nosh on? _____

23. ◯ Mall ◯ Outlet

24. Your absolute favorite article of clothing? _____

25. ◯ Frozen yogurt ◯ Ice cream?

26. What superpower would you love to have? _____

27. ◯ Potato chips ◯ French fries?

28. Cosmetic you can't live without? _____

29. Best teacher you ever had? _____

30. ◯ Spender ◯ Saver?

31. Who should play you in a movie version of your life? _____

32. If you were an animal, what would you be? _____

33. Best beverage? _____

34. Favorite cereal? _____

35. Who do you wish you could meet? _____

36. ◯ Fearful ◯ Fearless?

37. Which would you try? ◯ Skydiving ◯ Rappelling ◯ Scuba Diving

38. ◯ Butterflies ◯ Dragonflies?

39. ◯ Organic ◯ Junk food?

40. Favorite school subject? _____

1. What's your full name? . . . .

2. Elementary school: ☐ Bully ☐ Bullied?

3. Dream job? . . . .

4. Glass: ◯ ½ full ◯ ½ empty?

5. Ever broken a body part? ☐ Yep What? . . . . ☐ Nope

6. How many car accidents have you been in? . . . .

7. Ever caused a car accident? ◯ Yep ◯ Nope

8. Ever been sent to the principal's office? ☐ Yep ☐ Nope

9. Most beautiful (inside) person you know? . . . .

10. How do you relax? . . . .

11. ◯ Social butterfly ◯ Wallflower?

12. Your biggest question about life? . . . .

13. ☐ Secret keeper ☐ Blabbermouth?

14. What makes you cry? . . . .

15. Names of future children? Boy . . . . Girl . . . .

16. Who's your favorite relative? . . . .

17. What was your last dream? . . . .

18. What makes you crazy? . . . .

19. I wish I . . . .

20. ◯ Stick shift ◯ Automatic ◯ Can't drive yet?

21. Which appointment is worse? ☐ Doctor ☐ Dentist

22. Ever been to the emergency room? ◯ Yes ◯ No

23. ☐ Worry wart ☐ Worry free?

24. ◯ Bicycle through Europe ◯ African safari?

25. Favorite food court place? . . . .

26. ☐ Ice cubes ☐ Crushed ice?

27. What do you like on your burger? . . . .

28. Favorite fast food? . . . .

29. Favorite color of eyes? . . . .

30. Do you know sign language? ◯ YES ◯ NO

31. Favorite department store? . . . .

32. Who taught you to ride a bike? . . . .

33. How old were you when you learned to swim? . . . .

34. I would love to try . . . .

35. Who do you admire most? . . . .

36. ☐ Bikini ☐ Board shorts?

37. Worst movie ever? . . . .

38. Favorite kind of cookie? . . . .

39. Best commercial? . . . .

40. A word or phrase you say a lot? . . . .

1. First, middle, and last name? _ _ _ _ _ _ _ _ _ _ _ _ _ _ _ _ _

2. I can't live without _

3. Do you take vitamins? ☐ uh, yeah ☐ um, no

4. Do you floss? ☐ uh, yeah ☐ um, no

5. How many hair products do you use? ☐ 1 ☐ 2 ☐ 3 ☐ ?

6. Meanest thing you ever did to a sibling? _ _ _ _ _ _ _ _ _ _

7. Believe in UFOs? ☐ uh, yeah ☐ um, no

8. Can you identify constellations? ☐ uh, yeah ☐ um, no

9. ☐ Creamy ☐ Crunchy Peanut Butter?

10. Someone you miss? _

11. Believe in the Loch Ness Monster? ☐ uh, yeah ☐ um, no

12. Believe in Big Foot? ☐ uh, yeah ☐ um, no

13. Which would you pick? ☐ Extra $50 a week ☐ 3-day weekend

14. Any pets? ☐ uh, yeah _ _ _ _ _ _ _ _ _ _ _ _ ☐ um, no
                              (kind)

15. If yes to #14, names _ _ _ _ _ _ _ _ _ _ _ _ _ _ _ _ _ _

16. Museum of ☐ art ☐ natural history?

17. ☐ Train ☐ Plane ☐ Automobile?

18. I wish my hair _

19. Best amusement park ride? _ _ _ _ _ _ _ _ _ _ _ _ _ _ _ _

20. Best little kid movie? _ _ _ _ _ _ _ _ _ _ _ _ _ _ _ _ _ _

21. Favorite picture book? _ _ _ _ _ _ _ _ _ _ _ _ _ _ _ _

22. ☐ Apples ☐ Oranges?

23. ☐ Chocolate milk ☐ Soy milk ☐ Rice milk?

24. ☐ Hot dog ☐ Hamburger?

25. I wish someone would invent _ _ _ _ _ _ _ _ _ _ _ _ _ _

26. ☐ White ☐ Wheat?

27. Best era for fashion? ☐ '60s ☐ '70s ☐ '80s ☐ '90s ☐ now

28. How many hours per day online? _ _ _ _ _ _ _ _ _ _ _ _

29. How many hours per day on phone? _ _ _ _ _ _ _ _ _ _ _

30. Just say no to _ _ _ _ _ _ _ _ _ _ _ _ _ _ _ _ _ _

31. ☐ Flip-flops ☐ Strappy sandals?

32. Best food comes from which country? _ _ _ _ _ _ _ _ _ _

33. Run away from home when you were little? ☐ uh, yeah ☐ um, no

34. What's scarier? ☐ Snake ☐ Shark

35. What are you not good at? _ _ _ _ _ _ _ _ _ _ _ _ _ _

36. Friend you've had the longest? _ _ _ _ _ _ _ _ _ _ _ _

37. Friend who lives the farthest from you? _ _ _ _ _ _ _ _

38. Where does # 37 friend live? _ _ _ _ _ _ _ _ _ _ _ _ _

39. How many hours per day watching TV? _ _ _ _ _ _ _ _ _

40. Which one could you give up? ☐ E-mail ☐ Cell phone

1. First, middle, and last name? _____

2. What toothpaste do you use? _____

3. ◯ Shop alone ◯ Shop with mom ◯ Shop with friends?

4. Best type of cake? _____

5. I love the smell of _____

6. How do you like your popcorn? _____

7. Favorite magazine? _____

8. ◯ Aspirin ◯ Aceteminifin ◯ Ibuprofen ◯ Tough it out?

9. What did you do last night? _____

10. ◯ Manicure ◯ Do-it-yourself nails?

11. What's your favorite comfort food? _____

12. ◯ High fashion ◯ Total casual?

13. ◯ Kill bugs ◯ Try to save them?

14. Best friend in kindergarten? _____

15. I can't bear the sound of _____

16. What was your favorite thing on the playground? _____

17. I would love to see _____

18. I would love to time-travel back to _____

19. I would love to time-travel forward to _____

20. Can you change a tire? ◯ Yes ◯ No

21. Swallow anything by accident as a kid? ◯ Yes _____ ◯ No
    (what)

22. ◯ Romantic dinner for two   ◯ Big party?

23. Favorite take-out food? _____

24. I can't stand the smell of _____

25. Favorite smoothie? _____

26. Ever tried dog or cat food? ◯ Yes ◯ No

27. Hair color? _____

28. 👀 ◯ Contacts   ◯ Glasses   ◯ Great vision?

29. Favorite game as a kid? _____

30. ◯ Salty   ◯ Sweet?

31. I can't wait until I can _____

32. ◯ Lone Ranger   ◯ Team player?

33. Do you try to find shapes in clouds? ◯ Yes   ◯ No

34. ◯ Details ◯ Big picture?

35. What are you good at? _____

36. ◯ Favorite accessory? _____

37. ◯ Appointment for color   ◯ Dye your own hair?

38. I love to listen to _____

39. Coolest thing you learned this week? _____

40. ◯ Tap   ◯ Bottled   ◯ Sparkling water?

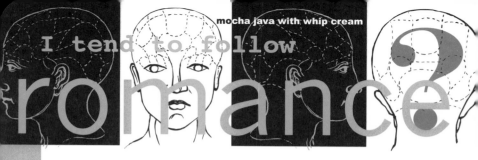

mocha java with whip cream

I tend to follow romance?

1. Name? _ _ _ _ _ _ _ _ _ _ _ _ _

2. ☐ Small talk ☐ Deep conversations?

3. ☐ Pilot ☐ Navigator?

4. Favorite ice cream flavor? _ _ _ _ _ _ _ _ _ _ _ _

5. I survived a ☐ hurricane ☐ tornado ☐ flood?

6. Favorite writer? _ _ _ _ _ _ _ _ _ _ _ _ _ _ _ _ _ _

7. Have you ever re-gifted? ☐ YES ☐ NO

8. ☐ Toilet-papered ☐ Toilet-paperer?

9. Favorite hot beverage? _ _ _ _ _ _ _ _ _ _ _ _ _ _

10. Time ☐ drags ☐ goes by too fast?

11. Most influential person in your life? _ _ _ _ _ _ _ _ _ _

12. Who would you be in a castle? ☐ Queen ☐ Princess ☐ Knight ☐ Jester

13. What do you daydream about? _ _ _ _ _ _ _ _ _ _ _ _ _

14. ☐ Meat eater ☐ Vegetarian ☐ Vegan?

15. Habit you wish you could change? _ _ _ _ _ _ _ _ _ _

16. Best type of movie? ☐ Romance ☐ Comedy ☐ Scary ☐ Action ☐ Sci-Fi

17. Any advice for a 5-year-old? _ _ _ _ _ _ _ _ _ _ _ _

18. ☐ Reality show ☐ Sitcom?

19. Birthday? _ _ _ _ _ _ _ _ _ _ _ _

20. ☐ Bagel ☐ Doughnut ☐ Croissant ☐ Cinnamon roll?

non-fat soy chai
I'm usually in the lead
sci-fi

21. ☐ ☀ Morning glory ☐ 🌙 Night owl?

22. Favorite forest animal? _ _ _ _ _ _ _ _ _ _ _ _ _ _ _ _ _

23. Birthmark? ☐ YES ☐ NO

24. 🍬 Favorite candy? _ _ _ _ _ _ _ _ _ _ _ _ _ _ _

25. ☐ Store-bought ☐ Homemade?

26. I don't understand _ _ _ _ _ _ _ _ _ _ _ _ _ _ _ _ _ _

27. Who would you be on a set? ☐ Director ☐ Star ☐ Supporting star ☐ Set designer

28. What food/beverage do you get at the movies? _ _ _ _ _ _ _ _ _ _

29. Favorite color for a car? _ _ _ _ _ _ _ _ _ _ _ _ _ _ _ _

30. It's not fair that _ _ _ _ _ _ _ _ _ _ _ _ _ _ _ _ _ _ _

31. Do you make your bed every morning? ☐ YES ☐ NO 🛏

32. 🕶 Favorite costume you've ever worn? _ _ _ _ _ _ _ _ _ _

33. Are you always up-to-date on current news? ☐ YES ☐ KIND OF ☐ NO

34. ☐ Waffle cone ☐ Sugar cone ☐ Cup?

35. Which is worse? ☐ No TV ☐ No music

36. ☐ Small purse ☐ Giant bag?

37. Favorite fairy tale? _ _ _ _ _ _ _ _ _ _ _ _ _ _ _ _ _ _

38. Ever have an imaginary friend? ☐ YES _ _ _ _ _ _ _ _ _ ☐ NO
                                          (Name)

39. Can different foods touch each other on your plate? ☐ YES ☐ NO

🐒 40. Best jungle animal? _ _ _ _ _ _ _ _ _ _ _ _ _ _ _

1. Name _____Where were you born? _____

2. Sit ◯ up front ◯ in the back?

3. Favorite toy when you were a kid? _____

4. Which is worse? ◯ Shopping for jeans ◯ Shopping for bikini

5. Favorite season and why? _____

6. Do you read the ending before you finish a book? ◯ Yes ◯ No

7. Best brand of jeans? _____

8. ◯ Island cabana ◯ European castle ◯ Safari tent ◯ Ski lodge

9. Favorite color combination? _____

10. ◯ Sunset ◯ Sunrise?

11. Favorite number? _____ Why? _____

12. Color your toes are painted? _____

13. Ever needed stitches? ◯ Yes Why? _____ ◯ No

14. My favorite shoes are _____

15. ◯ Right-handed ◯ Left-handed ◯ Ambidextrous?

16. How many children would you like someday? _____

17. ◯ Tent ◯ Cabin?

18. What scared you as a kid? _____

19. For just a day, I would switch places with _____

20. Wake up to ◯ alarm ◯ radio?

fire roasted with jalapeños
spicy
soak up the su

21. Been in a talent show? ◯ Yes Talent? _____ No ◯

22. ◯ Go with the flow   ◯ Stick to a routine?

23. Coolest first name? _____

24. ◯ Polka dots   ◯ Stripes   ◯ Plaid   ◯ Paisley?

25. Coolest last name? _____

26. ◯ Paper   ◯ Plastic?

27. What can you draw well? _____

28. ◯ Brownies   ◯ Chocolate chip cookies

29. I will not eat _____

30. ◯ Gold   ◯ Silver?

31. Favorite hangout? _____

32. How many times have you moved in your life? _____

33. As a kid, ◯ stuffed animal ◯ blankie?

34. Favorite thing to do on the weekend? _____

35. What color is your bedroom? _____

36. ◯ Mild   ◯ Spicy?

37. What would be hard to give up? _____

38. Cutest thing your pet does? _____

39. ◯ Shower   ◯ Bath?

40. I have a problem with _____

1. What is your full name? . . . .

2. Nickname? . . . .

3. ◯ Coke ◯ Pepsi?

4. Favorite song? . . . .

5. Earliest memory? . . . .

6. ◯ Milk ◯ Dark chocolate?

7. Who do you call when you're upset? . . . .

8. Do you recycle? ♻ ☐ yes ☐ no

9. ◯ Big Mac ◯ Whopper?

10. Last book you read? . . . .

11. ◯ 🏖 Beach ◯ ⛰ Mountains?

12. What kind of shoes are you wearing? . . . .

13. ◯ TV ◯ Book?

14. Favorite store? . . . .

15. What was the last thing you ate? 🍜 . . . .

16. ◯ Clean freak ◯ Total slob?

17. Favorite car? . . . .

18. Best gift you've ever received? . . . .

19. Best gift you've ever given? . . . .

20. Do you wish on ★ ★ ★ ? yes ☐ no ☐

21. Ever been stung by a jellyfish? ☐ yes ☐ no

22. Best cartoon ever? . . . .

23. What scares you? . . . .

24. Last person you spoke to? . . . .

25. Favorite doughnut? . . . .

26. Stupidest thing you've ever done? . . . .

27. Been to NYC? ☐ yes ☐ no

28. Best sitcom ever? . . . .

29. Been to LA? ☐ yes ☐ no

30. Favorite place you've visited? . . . .

31. Least favorite vegetable? . . . .

32. ◯ Dreamer ◯ Doer?

33. One word to describe you? . . . .

34. Name of your very first friend? . . . .

35. If I could, I would change my first name to . . . .

36. ◯ Night light ◯ Completely dark?

37. Ever pull an all-nighter? . . . .

38. Believe in love at first sight? ☐ yes ☐ no

39. Best toppings for pizza? . . . .

40. Ever owned a goldfish? ☐ yes name . . . . ☐ no

coke-or-pepsi.com

crazy

1. Name given at birth? _____

2. What do your friends call you? _____

3. What do you do when you're mad? _____

4. Favorite holiday and why? _____

5. Ever won anything? ☐ yeah What? _____ ☐ nah

6. What do you do on rainy days? ☂ _____

7. 🐕 ◯   🐈 ◯ person?

8. Favorite flower? _____

9. ◯ Coffee ◯ Tea?

10. Oldest living relative: 👵 Name _____ Age _____

11. Most annoying bug? _____

12. ◯ Tanning oil ◯ Sunscreen?

13. Nails: ◯ Painted ◯ Chipped ◯ Fake ◯ Bitten?

14. Wear painful shoes just because they're cute? ☐ yeah ☐ nah

15. Best type of music? _____

16. Ever been in love? ☐ yeah ☐ nah

17. Favorite actor? _____

18. ◯ Radio ◯ iPod?

19. Favorite actress? _____

20. Do you have a secret you've never told anyone? ☐ yeah ☐ nah

21. Did you ever believe in the Tooth Fairy? ☐ yeah ☐ nah

22. 🍕 Favorite thing to nosh on? _____

23. ◯ Mall ◯ Outlet

24. 🎀 Your absolute favorite article of clothing? _____

25. ◯ Frozen yogurt ◯ Ice cream?

26. What superpower would you love to have? _____

27. ◯ Potato chips ◯ French fries?

28. Cosmetic you can't live without? 💄 _____

29. Best teacher you ever had? _____

30. ◯ Spender ◯ Saver?

31. Who should play you in a movie version of your life? _____

32. If you were an animal, what would you be? 🐾 _____

33. 🥤 Best beverage? _____

34. Favorite cereal? _____

35. Who do you wish you could meet? _____

36. 🙈 ◯ Fearful 🙊 ◯ Fearless?

37. Which would you try? ◯ Skydiving ◯ Rappelling ◯ Scuba Diving

38. ◯ Butterflies ◯ Dragonflies?

39. 🫛 ◯ Organic ◯ Junk food? 🍬

40. Favorite school subject? _____

1. What's your full name? . . . .

2. Elementary school: ☐ Bully   ☐ Bullied?

3. Dream job? . . . .

4. Glass: ◯ ½ full   ◯ ½ empty?

5. Ever broken a body part? ☐ Yep What? . . . . ☐ Nope

6. How many car accidents have you been in? . . . .

7. Ever caused a car accident? ◯ Yep ◯ Nope

8. Ever been sent to the principal's office? ☐ Yep ☐ Nope

9. Most beautiful (inside) person you know? . . . .

10. How do you relax? . . . .

11. ◯ Social butterfly 🦋   ◯ Wallflower? 🌼

12. Your biggest question about life? . . . .

13. ☐ Secret keeper   ☐ Blabbermouth?

14. What makes you cry? . . . .

15. Names of future children? Boy . . . . Girl . . . .

16. Who's your favorite relative? . . . .

17. What was your last dream? . . . .

18. What makes you crazy? . . . .

19. I wish I . . . .

20. ◯ Stick shift ◯ Automatic ◯ Can't drive yet?

21. Which appointment is worse? ☐ Doctor ☐ Dentist

22. Ever been to the emergency room? ◯ Yes ◯ No

23. ☐ Worry wart ☐ Worry free?

24. ◯ Bicycle through Europe ◯ African safari?

25. Favorite food court place? . . . .

26. ☐ Ice cubes ☐ Crushed ice?

27. What do you like on your burger? . . . .

28. Favorite fast food? . . . .

29. Favorite color of eyes? . . . .

30. Do you know sign language? ◯ YES ◯ NO

31. Favorite department store? . . . .

32. Who taught you to ride a bike? . . . .

33. How old were you when you learned to swim? . . . .

34. I would love to try . . . .

35. Who do you admire most? . . . .

36. ☐ Bikini ☐ Board shorts?

37. Worst movie ever? . . . .

38. Favorite kind of cookie? . . . .

39. Best commercial? . . . .

40. A word or phrase you say a lot? . . . .

coke-or-pepsi.com

1. First, middle, and last name? _ _ _ _ _ _ _ _ _ _ _ _ _ _

2. I can't live without _ _ _ _ _ _ _ _ _ _ _ _ _ _ _ _ _ _

3. Do you take vitamins? ☐ uh, yeah ☐ um, no

4. Do you floss? ☐ uh, yeah ☐ um, no

5. How many hair products do you use? ☐ 1 ☐ 2 ☐ 3 ☐ ?

6. Meanest thing you ever did to a sibling? _ _ _ _ _ _ _ _ _

7. Believe in UFOs? ☐ uh, yeah ☐ um, no

8. Can you identify constellations? ☐ uh, yeah ☐ um, no

9. ☐ Creamy ☐ Crunchy Peanut Butter?

10. Someone you miss? _ _ _ _ _ _ _ _ _ _ _ _ _ _ _ _ _

11. Believe in the Loch Ness Monster? ☐ uh, yeah ☐ um, no

12. Believe in Big Foot? ☐ uh, yeah ☐ um, no

13. Which would you pick? ☐ Extra $50 a week ☐ 3-day weekend

14. Any pets? ☐ uh, yeah _ _ _ _ _ _ _ _ _ ☐ um, no
                              (kind)

15. If yes to #14, Names _ _ _ _ _ _ _ _ _ _ _ _ _ _ _ _

16. Museum of ☐ art ☐ natural history?

17. ☐ Train ☐ Plane ☐ Automobile?

18. I wish my hair _ _ _ _ _ _ _ _ _ _ _ _ _ _ _ _ _ _

19. Best amusement park ride? _ _ _ _ _ _ _ _ _ _ _ _ _

20. Best little kid movie? _ _ _ _ _ _ _ _ _ _ _ _ _ _ _

21. FAVORITE PICTURE BOOK? _ _ _ _ _ _ _ _ _

22. ☐ APPLES ☐ ORANGES?

23. ☐ CHOCOLATE MILK ☐ SOY MILK ☐ RICE MILK?

24. ☐ HOT DOG ☐ HAMBURGER?

25. I WISH SOMEONE WOULD INVENT _ _ _ _ _ _ _ _ _

26. ☐ WHITE ☐ WHEAT?

27. BEST ERA FOR FASHION? ☐ '60S ☐ '70S ☐ '80S ☐ '90S ☐ NOW

28. HOW MANY HOURS PER DAY ONLINE? _ _ _ _ _ _

29. HOW MANY HOURS PER DAY ON PHONE? _ _ _ _ _

30. JUST SAY NO TO _ _ _ _ _ _ _ _ _ _ _ _

31. ☐ FLIP-FLOPS ☐ STRAPPY SANDALS?

32. BEST FOOD COMES FROM WHICH COUNTRY? _ _ _ _ _

33. RUN AWAY FROM HOME WHEN YOU WERE LITTLE? ☐ UH, YEAH ☐ UM, NO

34. WHAT'S SCARIER? ☐ SNAKE ☐ SHARK

35. WHAT ARE YOU NOT GOOD AT? _ _ _ _ _ _ _ _

36. FRIEND YOU'VE HAD THE LONGEST? _ _ _ _ _ _ _

37. FRIEND WHO LIVES THE FARTHEST FROM YOU? _ _ _ _ _

38. WHERE DOES # 37 FRIEND LIVE? _ _ _ _ _ _ _

39. HOW MANY HOURS PER DAY WATCHING TV? _ _ _ _ _

40. WHICH ONE COULD YOU GIVE UP? ☐ E-MAIL ☐ CELL PHONE

coke-or-pepsi.com

1. First, middle, and last name? _____

2. What toothpaste do you use? _____

3. ◯ Shop alone ◯ Shop with mom ◯ Shop with friends?

4. Best type of cake? _____

5. I love the smell of _____

6. How do you like your popcorn? _____

7. Favorite magazine? _____

8. ◯ Aspirin ◯ Aceteminifin ◯ Ibuprofen ◯ Tough it out?

9. What did you do last night? _____

10. ◯ Manicure ◯ Do-it-yourself nails?

11. What's your favorite comfort food? _____

12. ◯ High fashion ◯ Total casual?

13. ◯ Kill bugs ◯ Try to save them?

14. Best friend in kindergarten? _____

15. I can't bear the sound of _____

16. What was your favorite thing on the playground? _____

17. I would love to see _____

18. I would love to time-travel back to _____

19. I would love to time-travel forward to _____

20. Can you change a tire? ◯ Yes ◯ No

head in the clouds
c h a o s
yang?

21. Swallow anything by accident as a kid? ◯ Yes _____ ◯ No
(what)

22. ◯ Romantic dinner for two ◯ Big party?

23. Favorite take-out food? _____

24. I can't stand the smell of 🙁 _____

25. Favorite smoothie? _____

26. Ever tried dog or cat food? ◯ Yes ◯ No

27. Hair color? _____

28. 👀 ◯ Contacts ◯ Glasses ◯ Great vision?

29. Favorite game as a kid? _____

30. ◯ Salty ◯ Sweet?

31. I can't wait until I can _____

32. ◯ Lone Ranger ◯ Team player?

33. Do you try to find shapes in clouds? ◯ Yes ◯ No ☁

34. ◯ Details ◯ Big picture?

35. What are you good at? _____

36. 📿 Favorite accessory? _____

37. ◯ Appointment for color ◯ Dye your own hair? 💿

38. I love to listen to _____

39. Coolest thing you learned this week? _____

40. ◯ Tap ◯ Bottled ◯ Sparkling water?

coke-or-pepsi.com

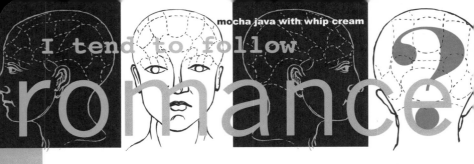

mocha java with whip cream

I tend to follow romance?

1. Name? _

2. ☐ Small talk ☐ Deep conversations?

3. ☐ Pilot ☐ Navigator?

4. Favorite ice cream flavor? _ _ _ _ _ _ _ _ _ _ _ _ _ _ _ _

5. I survived a ☐ hurricane ☐ tornado ☐ flood?

6. Favorite writer? _ _ _ _ _ _ _ _ _ _ _ _ _ _ _ _ _ _ _

7. Have you ever re-gifted? ☐ **YES** ☐ **NO**

8. ☐ Toilet-papered ☐ Toilet-paperer?

9. Favorite hot beverage? _ _ _ _ _ _ _ _ _ _ _ _ _ _ _ _ _

10. ☐ Time ☐ drags ☐ goes by too fast?

11. Most influential person in your life? _ _ _ _ _ _ _ _ _ _ _ _

12. Who would you be in a castle? ☐ Queen ☐ Princess ☐ Knight ☐ Jester

13. What do you daydream about? _ _ _ _ _ _ _ _ _ _ _ _ _ _

14. ☐ Meat eater ☐ Vegetarian ☐ Vegan?

15. Habit you wish you could change? _ _ _ _ _ _ _ _ _ _ _ _

16. Best type of movie? ☐ Romance ☐ Comedy ☐ Scary ☐ Action ☐ Sci-Fi

17. Any advice for a 5-year-old? _ _ _ _ _ _ _ _ _ _ _ _ _ _

18. ☐ Reality show ☐ Sitcom?

19. Birthday? _

20. ☐ Bagel ☐ Doughnut ☐ Croissant ☐ Cinnamon roll?

21. ⬜ ☀ Morning glory ⬜ 🌙 Night owl?

22. Favorite forest animal? _

23. Birthmark? ⬜ **YES** ⬜ **NO**

24. 🍬 Favorite candy? _ _ _ _ _ _ _ _ _ _ _ _ _ _ _ _ _ _ _

25. ⬜ Store–bought ⬜ Homemade?

26. I don't understand _

27. Who would you be on a set? ⬜ Director ⬜ Star ⬜ Supporting star ⬜ Set designer

28. What food/beverage do you get at the movies?_ _ _ _ _ _ _ _ _ _ _ _ _ _ _

29. Favorite color for a car? _

30. It's not fair that _

31. Do you make your bed every morning? ⬜ **YES** ⬜ **NO** 🛏

32. 🕷 Favorite costume you've ever worn? _ _ _ _ _ _ _ _ _ _ _ _

33. Are you always up-to-date on current news? ⬜ **YES** ⬜ **KIND OF** ⬜ **NO**

34. ⬜ Waffle cone ⬜ Sugar cone ⬜ Cup?

35. Which is worse? ⬜ No TV ⬜ No music

36. ⬜ Small purse ⬜ Giant bag?

37. Favorite fairy tale? _

38. Ever have an imaginary friend? ⬜ **YES** _ _ _ _ _ _ _ _ _ _ _ _ ⬜ **NO**
   (Name)

39. Can different foods touch each other on your plate? ⬜ **YES** ⬜ **NO**

🐒 40. Best jungle animal?_ _ _ _ _ _ _ _ _ _ _ _ _ _ _ _ _ _

1. Name _____ Where were you born? _____

2. Sit ◯ up front   ◯ in the back?

3. Favorite toy when you were a kid? _____

4. Which is worse? ◯ Shopping for jeans   ◯ Shopping for bikini

5. Favorite season and why? _____

6. Do you read the ending before you finish a book? ◯ Yes ◯ No

7. Best brand of jeans? _____

8. ◯ Island cabana ◯ European castle ◯ Safari tent ◯ Ski lodge

9. Favorite color combination? _____

10. ◯ Sunset ◯ Sunrise?

11. Favorite number? _____ Why? _____

12. Color your toes are painted? _____

13. Ever needed stitches? ◯ Yes Why? _____ ◯ No

14. My favorite shoes are _____

15. ◯ Right-handed   ◯ Left-handed   ◯ Ambidextrous?

16. How many children would you like someday? _____

17. ◯ Tent   ◯ Cabin?

18. What scared you as a kid? _____

19. For just a day, I would switch places with _____

20. Wake up to ◯ alarm ◯ radio?

21. Been in a talent show? ○ Yes Talent? _____ No ○

22. ○ Go with the flow ○ Stick to a routine?

23. Coolest first name? _____

24. ○ Polka dots ○ Stripes ○ Plaid ○ Paisley?

25. Coolest last name? _____

26. ○ Paper ○ Plastic?

27. What can you draw well? _____

28. ○ Brownies ○ Chocolate chip cookies

29. I will not eat _____

30. ○ Gold ○ Silver?

31. Favorite hangout? _____

32. How many times have you moved in your life? _____

33. As a kid, ○ stuffed animal ○ blankie?

34. Favorite thing to do on the weekend? _____

35. What color is your bedroom? _____

36. ○ Mild ○ Spicy?

37. What would be hard to give up? _____

38. Cutest thing your pet does? _____

39. ○ Shower ○ Bath?

40. I have a problem with _____

1. What is your full name? . . . .

2. Nickname? . . . .

3. ◯ Coke ◯ Pepsi?

4. Favorite song? . . . .

5. Earliest memory? . . . .

6. ◯ Milk ◯ Dark chocolate?

7. Who do you call when you're upset? . . . .

8. Do you recycle? ♲ ☐ yes ☐ no

9. ◯ Big Mac ◯ Whopper?

10. Last book you read? . . . .

11. ◯ 🚲 Beach ◯ ⛰ Mountains?

12. What kind of shoes are you wearing? . . . .

13. ◯ TV ◯ Book?

14. Favorite store? . . . .

15. What was the last thing you ate? 🍜 . . . .

16. ◯ Clean freak ◯ Total slob?

17. Favorite car? . . . .

18. Best gift you've ever received? . . . .

19. Best gift you've ever given? . . . .

20. Do you wish on ★ ★ ★ ? yes ☐ no ☐

NO
PARKING

public knowledge

my room is always perfect

21. Ever been stung by a jellyfish? ☐ yes ☐ no

22. Best cartoon ever? . . . .

23. What scares you? . . . .

24. Last person you spoke to? . . . .

25. Favorite doughnut? . . . .

26. Stupidest thing you've ever done? . . . .

27. Been to NYC? ☐ yes ☐ no

28. Best sitcom ever? . . . .

29. Been to LA? ☐ yes ☐ no

30. Favorite place you've visited? . . . .

31. Least favorite vegetable? . . . .

32. ◯ Dreamer ◯ Doer?

33. One word to describe you? . . . .

34. Name of your very first friend? . . . .

35. If I could, I would change my first name to . . . .

36. ◯ Night light ◯ Completely dark?

37. Ever pull an all-nighter? . . . .

38. Believe in love at first sight? ☐ yes ☐ no

39. Best toppings for pizza? . . . .

40. Ever owned a goldfish? ☐ yes name . . . . ☐ no

coke-or-pepsi.com

crazy

1. Name given at birth? _____

2. What do your friends call you? _____

3. What do you do when you're mad? _____

4. Favorite holiday and why? _____

5. Ever won anything? ☐ *yeah* What? _____ ☐ *nah*

6. What do you do on rainy days? ☂ _____

7. 🐕 ◯ 🐈 ◯ person?

8. Favorite flower? _____

9. ◯ Coffee ◯ Tea?

10. Oldest living relative: 👴 Name _____ Age _____

11. Most annoying bug? _____

12. ◯ Tanning oil ◯ Sunscreen?

13. Nails: ◯ Painted ◯ Chipped ◯ Fake ◯ Bitten?

14. Wear painful shoes just because they're cute? ☐ *yeah* ☐ *nah*

15. Best type of music? _____

16. Ever been in love? ☐ *yeah* ☐ *nah*

17. Favorite actor? _____

18. ◯ Radio ◯ iPod?

19. Favorite actress? _____

20. Do you have a secret you've never told anyone? ☐ *yeah* ☐ *nah*

21. Did you ever believe in the Tooth Fairy? ☐ yeah ☐ nah

22. 🍕 Favorite thing to nosh on? _____

23. ◯ Mall ◯ Outlet

24. 🎀 Your absolute favorite article of clothing? _____

25. ◯ Frozen yogurt ◯ Ice cream?

26. What superpower would you love to have? _____

27. ◯ Potato chips ◯ French fries?

28. Cosmetic you can't live without? 🪞 _____

29. Best teacher you ever had? _____

30. ◯ Spender ◯ Saver?

31. Who should play you in a movie version of your life? _____

32. If you were an animal, what would you be? _____

33. 🥫 Best beverage? _____

34. Favorite cereal? _____

35. Who do you wish you could meet? _____

36. 😨 ◯ Fearful 😁 ◯ Fearless?

37. Which would you try? ◯ Skydiving ◯ Rappelling ◯ Scuba Diving

38. ◯ Butterflies ◯ Dragonflies?

39. 🫛 ◯ Organic ◯ Junk food? 🍬

40. Favorite school subject? _____

1. What's your full name? . . . .

2. Elementary school: ☐ Bully ☐ Bullied?

3. Dream job? . . . .

4. Glass: ◯ ½ full ◯ ½ empty?

5. Ever broken a body part? ☐ Yep What? . . . . ☐ Nope

6. How many car accidents have you been in? . . . .

7. Ever caused a car accident? ◯ Yep ◯ Nope

8. Ever been sent to the principal's office? ☐ Yep ☐ Nope

9. Most beautiful (inside) person you know? . . . .

10. How do you relax? . . . .

11. ◯ Social butterfly 🦋 ◯ Wallflower? 🌼

12. Your biggest question about life? . . . .

13. ☐ Secret keeper ☐ Blabbermouth?

14. What makes you cry? . . . .

15. Names of future children? Boy . . . . Girl . . . .

16. Who's your favorite relative? . . . .

17. What was your last dream? . . . .

18. What makes you crazy? . . . .

19. I wish I . . . .

20. ◯ Stick shift ◯ Automatic ◯ Can't drive yet?

21. Which appointment is worse? ☐ Doctor ☐ Dentist

22. Ever been to the emergency room? ◯ Yes ◯ No

23. ☐ Worry wart ☐ Worry free?

24. ◯ Bicycle through Europe ◯ African safari?

25. Favorite food court place? . . . .

26. ☐ Ice cubes ☐ Crushed ice?

27. What do you like on your burger? . . . .

28. Favorite fast food? . . . .

29. Favorite color of eyes? . . . .

30. Do you know sign language? ◯ YES ◯ NO

31. Favorite department store? . . . .

32. Who taught you to ride a bike? . . . .

33. How old were you when you learned to swim? . . . .

34. I would love to try . . . .

35. Who do you admire most? . . . .

36. ☐ Bikini ☐ Board shorts?

37. Worst movie ever? . . . .

38. Favorite kind of cookie? . . . .

39. Best commercial? . . . .

40. A word or phrase you say a lot? . . . .

1. First, middle, and last name? _ _ _ _ _ _ _ _ _ _ _ _ _ _ _ _ _ _

2. I can't live without _ .

3. Do you take vitamins? ☐ uh, yeah ☐ um, no

4. Do you floss? ☐ uh, yeah ☐ um, no

5. How many hair products do you use? ☐ 1 ☐ 2 ☐ 3 ☐ ?

6. Meanest thing you ever did to a sibling? _ _ _ _ _ _ _ _ _ _ .

7. Believe in UFOs? ☐ uh, yeah ☐ um, no

8. Can you identify constellations? ☐ uh, yeah ☐ um, no

9. ☐ Creamy ☐ Crunchy Peanut Butter?

10. Someone you miss? _ _ _ _ _ _ _ _ _ _ _ _ _ _ _ _ _ _ _

11. Believe in the Loch Ness Monster? ☐ uh, yeah ☐ um, no

12. Believe in Big Foot? ☐ uh, yeah ☐ um, no

13. Which would you pick? ☐ Extra $50 a week ☐ 3-day weekend

14. Any pets? ☐ uh, yeah _ _ _ _ _ _ _ _ _ _ _ _ ☐ um, no
                              (kind)

15. If yes to #14, Names _ _ _ _ _ _ _ _ _ _ _ _ _ _ _ _ _ _

16. Museum of ☐ art ☐ natural history?

17. ☐ Train ☐ Plane ☐ Automobile?

18. I wish my hair _

19. Best amusement park ride? _ _ _ _ _ _ _ _ _ _ _ _ _ _

20. Best little kid movie? _ _ _ _ _ _ _ _ _ _ _ _ _ _ _

21. FAVORITE PICTURE BOOK? _ _ _ _ _ _ _ _ _ _ _ _ _ _ _

22. ☐ APPLES ☐ ORANGES?

23. ☐ CHOCOLATE MILK ☐ SOY MILK ☐ RICE MILK?

24. ☐ HOT DOG ☐ HAMBURGER?

25. I WISH SOMEONE WOULD INVENT _ _ _ _ _ _ _ _ _ _ _ _

26. ☐ WHITE ☐ WHEAT?

27. BEST ERA FOR FASHION? ☐ '60S ☐ '70S ☐ '80S ☐ '90S ☐ NOW

28. HOW MANY HOURS PER DAY ONLINE? _ _ _ _ _ _ _ _ _ _

29. HOW MANY HOURS PER DAY ON PHONE? _ _ _ _ _ _ _ _ _

30. JUST SAY NO TO _ _ _ _ _ _ _ _ _ _ _ _ _ _ _ _ _

31. ☐ FLIP-FLOPS ☐ STRAPPY SANDALS?

32. BEST FOOD COMES FROM WHICH COUNTRY? _ _ _ _ _ _ _ _

33. RUN AWAY FROM HOME WHEN YOU WERE LITTLE? ☐ UH, YEAH ☐ UM, NO

34. WHAT'S SCARIER? ☐ SNAKE ☐ SHARK

35. WHAT ARE YOU NOT GOOD AT? _ _ _ _ _ _ _ _ _ _ _ _ _

36. FRIEND YOU'VE HAD THE LONGEST? _ _ _ _ _ _ _ _ _ _ _

37. FRIEND WHO LIVES THE FARTHEST FROM YOU? _ _ _ _ _ _ _

38. WHERE DOES # 37 FRIEND LIVE? _ _ _ _ _ _ _ _ _ _ _ _

39. HOW MANY HOURS PER DAY WATCHING TV? _ _ _ _ _ _ _ _

40. WHICH ONE COULD YOU GIVE UP? ☐ E-MAIL ☐ CELL PHONE

? **yin**
feet planted on the ground
c a l m

1. First, middle, and last name? _____

2. What toothpaste do you use? _____

3. ◯ Shop alone   ◯ Shop with mom   ◯ Shop with friends?

4. Best type of cake? _____

5. I love the smell of _____

6. How do you like your popcorn? _____

7. Favorite magazine? _____

8. ◯ Aspirin ◯ Aceteminifin ◯ Ibuprofen ◯ Tough it out?

9. What did you do last night? _____

10. ◯ Manicure   ◯ Do-it-yourself nails?

11. What's your favorite comfort food? _____

12. ◯ High fashion ◯ Total casual?

13. ◯ Kill bugs ◯ Try to save them?

14. Best friend in kindergarten? _____

15. I can't bear the sound of _____

16. What was your favorite thing on the playground? _____

17. I would love to see _____

18. I would love to time-travel back to _____

19. I would love to time-travel forward to _____

20. Can you change a tire? ◯ Yes ◯ No

yang?
head in the clouds
c h a o s

21. Swallow anything by accident as a kid? ◯ Yes _____ (what) ◯ No

22. ◯ Romantic dinner for two ◯ Big party?

23. Favorite take-out food? _____

24. I can't stand the smell of _____

25. Favorite smoothie? _____

26. Ever tried dog or cat food? ◯ Yes ◯ No

27. Hair color? _____

28. ◯ Contacts ◯ Glasses ◯ Great vision?

29. Favorite game as a kid? _____

30. ◯ Salty ◯ Sweet?

31. I can't wait until I can _____

32. ◯ Lone Ranger ◯ Team player?

33. Do you try to find shapes in clouds? ◯ Yes ◯ No

34. ◯ Details ◯ Big picture?

35. What are you good at? _____

36. Favorite accessory? _____

37. ◯ Appointment for color ◯ Dye your own hair?

38. I love to listen to _____

39. Coolest thing you learned this week? _____

40. ◯ Tap ◯ Bottled ◯ Sparkling water?

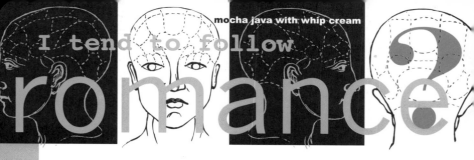

mocha java with whip cream

I tend to follow romance?

1. Name? _

2. ☐ Small talk ☐ Deep conversations?

3. ☐ Pilot ☐ Navigator?

4. Favorite ice cream flavor? _ _ _ _ _ _ _ _ _ _ _ _ _

5. I survived a ☐ hurricane ☐ tornado ☐ flood?

6. Favorite writer? _ _ _ _ _ _ _ _ _ _ _

7. Have you ever re-gifted? ☐ **YES** ☐ **NO**

8. ☐ Toilet-papered ☐ Toilet-paperer?

9. Favorite hot beverage? _ _ _ _ _ _ _ _ _ _ _ _ _ _ _ _ _

10. Time ☐ drags ☐ goes by too fast?

11. Most influential person in your life? _ _ _ _ _ _ _ _ _

12. Who would you be in a castle? ☐ Queen ☐ Princess ☐ Knight ☐ Jester

13. What do you daydream about? _ _ _ _ _ _ _ _ _ _ _ _

14. ☐ Meat eater ☐ Vegetarian ☐ Vegan?

15. Habit you wish you could change? _ _ _ _ _ _ _ _ _

16. Best type of movie? ☐ Romance ☐ Comedy ☐ Scary ☐ Action ☐ Sci-Fi

17. Any advice for a 5-year-old? _ _ _ _ _ _ _ _ _ _ _ _ _

18. ☐ Reality show ☐ Sitcom?

19. Birthday? _ _ _ _ _ _ _ _ _ _ _ _ _ _ _ _

20. ☐ Bagel ☐ Doughnut ☐ Croissant ☐ Cinnamon roll?

21. ☐ ☀ Morning glory ☐ 🌙 Night owl?

22. Favorite forest animal? _ _ _ _ _ _ _ _ _ _ _ _ _ _ _

23. Birthmark? ☐ **YES** ☐ **NO**

24. 🍬 Favorite candy? _ _ _ _ _ _ _ _ _ _ _ _ _ _

25. ☐ Store-bought ☐ Homemade?

26. I don't understand _ _ _ _ _ _ _ _ _ _ _ _ _ _ _ _ _

27. Who would you be on a set? ☐ Director ☐ Star ☐ Supporting star ☐ Set designer

28. What food/beverage do you get at the movies? _ _ _ _ _ _ _ _ _ _ _

29. Favorite color for a car? _ _ _ _ _ _ _ _ _ _ _ _ _

30. It's not fair that _ _ _ _ _ _ _ _ _ _ _ _ _ _ _ _

31. Do you make your bed every morning? ☐ **YES** ☐ **NO**

32. 👓 Favorite costume you've ever worn? _ _ _ _ _ _ _ _ _ _ _

33. Are you always up-to-date on current news? ☐ **YES** ☐ **KIND OF** ☐ **NO**

34. ☐ Waffle cone ☐ Sugar cone ☐ Cup?

35. Which is worse? ☐ No TV ☐ No music

36. ☐ Small purse ☐ Giant bag?

37. Favorite fairy tale? _ _ _ _ _ _ _ _ _ _ _ _ _ _ _

38. Ever have an imaginary friend? ☐ **YES** _ _ _ _ _ _ _ _ _ ☐ **NO**
                                              (Name)

39. Can different foods touch each other on your plate? ☐ **YES** ☐ **NO**

🐵 40. Best jungle animal? _ _ _ _ _ _ _ _ _ _ _ _ _ _

coke-or-pepsi.com

1. Name _____ Where were you born? _____
2. Sit ○ up front   ○ in the back?
3. Favorite toy when you were a kid? _____
4. Which is worse? ○ Shopping for jeans   ○ Shopping for bikini
5. Favorite season and why? _____
6. Do you read the ending before you finish a book?   ○ Yes   ○ No
7. Best brand of jeans? _____
8. ○ Island cabana ○ European castle ○ Safari tent ○ Ski lodge
9. Favorite color combination? _____
10. ○ Sunset   ○ Sunrise?
11. Favorite number? _____ Why? _____
12. Color your toes are painted? _____
13. Ever needed stitches? ○ Yes Why? _____ ○ No
14. My favorite shoes are _____
15. ○ Right-handed   ○ Left-handed   ○ Ambidextrous?
16. How many children would you like someday? _____
17. ○ Tent   ○ Cabin?
18. What scared you as a kid? _____
19. For just a day, I would switch places with _____
20. Wake up to ○ alarm   ○ radio?

fire roasted with jalapeños

spicy

soak up the su

21. Been in a talent show? ◯ Yes Talent? _____ No ◯

22. ◯ Go with the flow   ◯ Stick to a routine?

23. Coolest first name? _____

24. ◯ Polka dots ◯ Stripes ◯ Plaid ◯ Paisley?

25. Coolest last name? _____

26. ◯ Paper ◯ Plastic?

27. What can you draw well? _____

28. ◯ Brownies ◯ Chocolate chip cookies

29. I will not eat _____

30. ◯ Gold ◯ Silver?

31. Favorite hangout? _____

32. How many times have you moved in your life? _____

33. As a kid, ◯ stuffed animal ◯ blankie?

34. Favorite thing to do on the weekend? _____

35. What color is your bedroom? _____

36. ◯ Mild ◯ Spicy?

37. What would be hard to give up? _____

38. Cutest thing your pet does? _____

39. ◯ Shower ◯ Bath?

40. I have a problem with _____

1. What is your full name? . . . .

2. Nickname? . . . .

3. ◯ Coke ◯ Pepsi?

4. Favorite song? . . . .

5. Earliest memory? . . . .

6. ◯ Milk ◯ Dark chocolate?

7. Who do you call when you're upset? . . . .

8. Do you recycle? ♻ ☐ yes ☐ no

9. ◯ Big Mac ◯ Whopper?

10. Last book you read? . . . .

11. ◯ 🏖 Beach ◯ 🏔 Mountains?

12. What kind of shoes are you wearing? . . . .

13. ◯ TV ◯ Book?

14. Favorite store? . . . .

15. What was the last thing you ate? 🍜 . . . .

16. ◯ Clean freak ◯ Total slob?

17. Favorite car? . . . .

18. Best gift you've ever received? . . . .

19. Best gift you've ever given? . . . .

20. Do you wish on ★ ★ ★ ? yes ☐ no ☐

21. Ever been stung by a jellyfish? ☐ yes ☐ no

22. Best cartoon ever? . . . .

23. What scares you? . . . .

24. Last person you spoke to? . . . .

25. Favorite doughnut? . . . .

26. Stupidest thing you've ever done? . . . .

27. Been to NYC? ☐ yes ☐ no

28. Best sitcom ever? . . . .

29. Been to LA? ☐ yes ☐ no

30. Favorite place you've visited? . . . .

31. Least favorite vegetable? . . . .

32. ◯ Dreamer ◯ Doer?

33. One word to describe you? . . . .

34. Name of your very first friend? . . . .

35. If I could, I would change my first name to . . . .

36. ◯ Night light ◯ Completely dark?

37. Ever pull an all-nighter? . . . .

38. Believe in love at first sight? ☐ yes ☐ no

39. Best toppings for pizza? . . . .

40. Ever owned a goldfish? ☐ yes name . . . . ☐ no

1. Name given at birth? _____

2. What do your friends call you? _____

3. What do you do when you're mad? _____

4. Favorite holiday and why? _____

5. Ever won anything? ☐ *yeah* What? _____ ☐ *nah*

6. What do you do on rainy days? ☂ _____

7. 🐕 ◯ 🐈 ◯ person?

8. Favorite flower? _____

9. ◯ Coffee ◯ Tea?

10. Oldest living relative: 👵 Name _____ Age _____

11. Most annoying bug? _____

12. ◯ Tanning oil ◯ Sunscreen?

13. Nails: ◯ Painted ◯ Chipped ◯ Fake ◯ Bitten?

14. Wear painful shoes just because they're cute? ☐ *yeah* ☐ *nah*

15. Best type of music? _____

16. Ever been in love? ☐ *yeah* ☐ *nah*

17. Favorite actor? _____

18. ◯ Radio ◯ iPod?

19. Favorite actress? _____

20. Do you have a secret you've never told anyone? ☐ *yeah* ☐ *nah*

21. Did you ever believe in the Tooth Fairy? ☐ *yeah* ☐ *nah*

22. 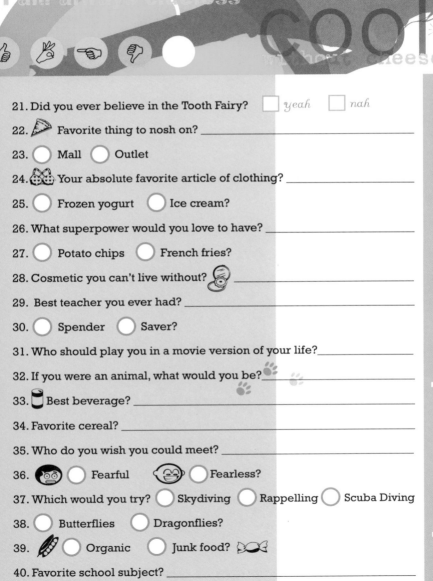 Favorite thing to nosh on? _____

23. ◯ Mall ◯ Outlet

24. Your absolute favorite article of clothing? _____

25. ◯ Frozen yogurt ◯ Ice cream?

26. What superpower would you love to have? _____

27. ◯ Potato chips ◯ French fries?

28. Cosmetic you can't live without? _____

29. Best teacher you ever had? _____

30. ◯ Spender ◯ Saver?

31. Who should play you in a movie version of your life? _____

32. If you were an animal, what would you be? _____

33. Best beverage? _____

34. Favorite cereal? _____

35. Who do you wish you could meet? _____

36. ◯ Fearful ◯ Fearless?

37. Which would you try? ◯ Skydiving ◯ Rappelling ◯ Scuba Diving

38. ◯ Butterflies ◯ Dragonflies?

39. ◯ Organic ◯ Junk food?

40. Favorite school subject? _____

1. What's your full name? . . . .

2. Elementary school: ☐ Bully ☐ Bullied?

3. Dream job? . . . .

4. Glass: ◯ ½ full ◯ ½ empty?

5. Ever broken a body part? ☐ Yep What? . . . . ☐ Nope

6. How many car accidents have you been in? . . . .

7. Ever caused a car accident? ◯ Yep ◯ Nope

8. 😟 Ever been sent to the principal's office? ☐ Yep ☐ Nope

9. Most beautiful (inside) person you know? . . . .

10. How do you relax? . . . .

11. ◯ Social butterfly 🦋 ◯ Wallflower? 🌼

12. Your biggest question about life? . . . .

13. ☐ Secret keeper ☐ Blabbermouth?

14. What makes you cry? . . . .

15. 👶 Names of future children? Boy . . . . Girl . . . .

16. Who's your favorite relative? . . . .

17. 🌙 What was your last dream? . . . .

18. What makes you crazy? 😫 . . . .

19. I wish I . . . .

20. ◯ Stick shift ◯ Automatic ◯ Can't drive yet?

21. Which appointment is worse? ☐ Doctor ☐ Dentist

22. Ever been to the emergency room? ◯ Yes ◯ No

23. ☐ Worry wart ☐ Worry free?

24. ◯ Bicycle through Europe ◯ African safari?

25. Favorite food court place? . . . .

26. ☐ Ice cubes ☐ Crushed ice?

27. 🍔 What do you like on your burger? . . . .

28. Favorite fast food? . . . .

29. Favorite color of eyes? . . . .

30. Do you know sign language? ◯ Yes ◯ No

31. Favorite department store? . . . .

32. Who taught you to ride a bike? 🚲 . . . .

33. How old were you when you learned to swim? . . . .

34. I would love to try . . . .

35. Who do you admire most? . . . .

36. ☐ Bikini ☐ Board shorts?

37. Worst movie ever? . . . .

38. Favorite kind of cookie? . . . .

39. Best commercial? 📺 . . . .

40. A word or phrase you say a lot? . . . .

1. First, middle, and last name? _ _ _ _ _ _ _ _ _ _ _ _ _ _ _ _ _

2. I can't live without _ .

3. Do you take vitamins? ☐ uh, yeah ☐ um, no

4. Do you floss? ☐ uh, yeah ☐ um, no

5. How many hair products do you use? ☐ 1 ☐ 2 ☐ 3 ☐ ?

6. Meanest thing you ever did to a sibling? _ _ _ _ _ _ _ _ _ _ .

7. Believe in UFOs? ☐ uh, yeah ☐ um, no

8. Can you identify constellations? ☐ uh, yeah ☐ um, no

9. ☐ Creamy ☐ Crunchy Peanut Butter?

10. Someone you miss? _

11. Believe in the Loch Ness Monster? ☐ uh, yeah ☐ um, no

12. Believe in Big Foot? ☐ uh, yeah ☐ um, no

13. Which would you pick? ☐ Extra $50 a week ☐ 3-day weekend

14. Any pets? ☐ uh, yeah _ _ _ _ _ _ _ _ _ _ _ _ ☐ um, no
                              (kind)

15. If yes to #14, Names _ _ _ _ _ _ _ _ _ _ _ _ _ _ _ _ _ _ _

16. Museum of ☐ art ☐ natural history?

17. ☐ Train ☐ Plane ☐ Automobile?

18. I wish my hair _

19. Best amusement park ride? _ _ _ _ _ _ _ _ _ _ _ _ _ _ _ _ _

20. Best little kid movie? _ _ _ _ _ _ _ _ _ _ _ _ _ _ _ _ _ _ _

It's all about the fun time

woof ?

BELIEVE IN YOUR FRIENDS

21. FAVORITE PICTURE BOOK? _ _ _ _ _ _ _ _ _ _ _ _ _

22. ☐ APPLES ☐ ORANGES?

23. ☐ CHOCOLATE MILK ☐ SOY MILK ☐ RICE MILK?

24. ☐ HOT DOG ☐ HAMBURGER?

25. I WISH SOMEONE WOULD INVENT _ _ _ _ _ _ _ _ _ _ _

26. ☐ WHITE ☐ WHEAT?

27. BEST ERA FOR FASHION? ☐ '60S ☐ '70S ☐ '80S ☐ '90S ☐ NOW

28. HOW MANY HOURS PER DAY ONLINE? _ _ _ _ _ _ _ _

29. HOW MANY HOURS PER DAY ON PHONE? _ _ _ _ _ _ _

30. JUST SAY NO TO _ _ _ _ _ _ _ _ _ _ _

31. ☐ FLIP-FLOPS ☐ STRAPPY SANDALS?

32. BEST FOOD COMES FROM WHICH COUNTRY? _ _ _ _ _ _

33. RUN AWAY FROM HOME WHEN YOU WERE LITTLE? ☐ UH, YEAH ☐ UM, NO

34. WHAT'S SCARIER? ☐ SNAKE ☐ SHARK

35. WHAT ARE YOU NOT GOOD AT? _ _ _ _ _ _ _ _

36. FRIEND YOU'VE HAD THE LONGEST? _ _ _ _ _ _ _

37. FRIEND WHO LIVES THE FARTHEST FROM YOU? _ _ _ _

38. WHERE DOES # 37 FRIEND LIVE? _ _ _ _ _ _ _ _

39. HOW MANY HOURS PER DAY WATCHING TV? _ _ _ _ _

40. WHICH ONE COULD YOU GIVE UP? ☐ E-MAIL ☐ CELL PHONE

yin

feet planted on the ground

c a l m

?

1. First, middle, and last name? _____

2. What toothpaste do you use? _____

3. ( ) Shop alone ( ) Shop with mom ( ) Shop with friends?

4. Best type of cake? _____

5. I love the smell of _____

6. How do you like your popcorn? _____

7. Favorite magazine? _____

8. ( ) Aspirin ( ) Aceteminifin ( ) Ibuprofen ( ) Tough it out?

9. What did you do last night? _____

10. ( ) Manicure ( ) Do-it-yourself nails?

11. What's your favorite comfort food? _____

12. ( ) High fashion ( ) Total casual?

13. ( ) Kill bugs ( ) Try to save them?

14. Best friend in kindergarten? _____

15. I can't bear the sound of _____

16. What was your favorite thing on the playground? _____

17. I would love to see _____

18. I would love to time-travel back to _____

19. I would love to time-travel forward to _____

20. Can you change a tire? ( ) Yes ( ) No

c h a o s

21. Swallow anything by accident as a kid? ◯ Yes _____ ◯ No
(what)

22. ◯ Romantic dinner for two ◯ Big party?

23. Favorite take-out food? _____

24. I can't stand the smell of 😣 _____

25. Favorite smoothie? _____

26. Ever tried dog or cat food? ◯ Yes ◯ No

27. Hair color? _____

28. 👀 ◯ Contacts ◯ Glasses ◯ Great vision?

29. Favorite game as a kid? _____

30. ◯ Salty ◯ Sweet?

31. I can't wait until I can _____

32. ◯ Lone Ranger ◯ Team player?

33. Do you try to find shapes in clouds? ◯ Yes ◯ No

34. ◯ Details ◯ Big picture?

35. What are you good at? _____

36. 💍 Favorite accessory? _____

37. ◯ Appointment for color ◯ Dye your own hair?

38. I love to listen to _____

39. Coolest thing you learned this week? _____

40. ◯ Tap ◯ Bottled ◯ Sparkling water?

-pepsi.com

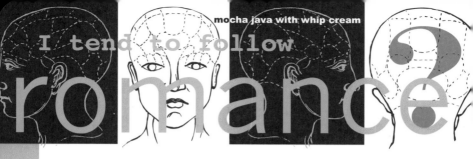

mocha java with whip cream

I tend to follow romance?

1. Name? _ _ _ _ _ _ _ _ _ _ _ _ _ _ _ _

2. ☐ Small talk ☐ Deep conversations?

3. ☐ Pilot ☐ Navigator?

4. Favorite ice cream flavor? _ _ _ _ _ _ _ _ _

5. I survived a ☐ hurricane ☐ tornado ☐ flood?

6. Favorite writer? _ _ _ _ _ _ _ _ _ _ _ _ _

7. Have you ever re-gifted? ☐ **YES** ☐ **NO**

8. ☐ Toilet-papered ☐ Toilet-paperer?

9. Favorite hot beverage? _ _ _ _ _ _ _ _ _ _ _ _ _ _ _ _

10. ⏰ Time ☐ drags ☐ goes by too fast?

11. Most influential person in your life? _ _ _ _ _ _ _ _ _ _

12. Who would you be in a castle? ☐ Queen ☐ Princess ☐ Knight ☐ Jester

13. What do you daydream about? ☺ _ _ _ _ _ _ _ _ _ _ _ _ _

14. ☐ Meat eater ☐ Vegetarian ☐ Vegan?

15. Habit you wish you could change? _ _ _ _ _ _ _ _ _ _ _ _

16. Best type of movie? ☐ Romance ☐ Comedy ☐ Scary ☐ Action ☐ Sci-Fi

17. Any advice for a 5-year-old? _ _ _ _ _ _ _ _ _ _ _ _ _ _

18. ☐ Reality show ☐ Sitcom?

19. Birthday? _ _ _ _ _ _ _ _ _ _ _ _ _ _

20. ☐ Bagel ☐ Doughnut ☐ Croissant ☐ Cinnamon roll?

21. ☐ ☀ Morning glory ☐ 🌙 Night owl?

22. Favorite forest animal? _ _ _ _ _ _ _ _ _ _ _ _ _ _ _ _ _ _

23. Birthmark? ☐ **YES** ☐ **NO**

24. 🍬 Favorite candy? _ _ _ _ _ _ _ _ _ _ _ _ _

25. ☐ Store–bought ☐ Homemade?

26. I don't understand _ _ _ _ _ _ _ _ _ _ _ _ _ _ _ _ _

27. Who would you be on a set? ☐ Director ☐ Star ☐ Supporting star ☐ Set designer

28. What food/beverage do you get at the movies?_ _ _ _ _ _ _ _ _ _ _ _

29. Favorite color for a car? _ _ _ _ _ _ _ _ _ _ _ _ _ _

30. It's not fair that _ _ _ _ _ _ _ _ _ _ _ _ _ _ _ _ _ _ _

31. Do you make your bed every morning? ☐ **YES** ☐ **NO**

32. 👓 Favorite costume you've ever worn? _ _ _ _ _ _ _ _

33. Are you always up–to–date on current news? ☐ **YES** ☐ **KIND OF** ☐ **NO**

34. ☐ Waffle cone ☐ Sugar cone ☐ Cup?

35. Which is worse? ☐ No TV ☐ No music

36. ☐ Small purse ☐ Giant bag?

37. Favorite fairy tale? _

38. Ever have an imaginary friend? ☐ **YES** _ _ _ _ _ _ _ _ ☐ **NO**
                                                    (Name)

39. Can different foods touch each other on your plate? ☐ **YES** ☐ **NO**

40. Best jungle animal?_ _ _ _ _ _ _ _ _ _ _ _ _ _ _ _ _ _ _

Check out
coke-or-pepsi.com

Get more questions

Shop the online store for
cool new merchandise!

coke OR
pepsi?